THE DESTROYED WORLD AND THE GUILTY SELF

THE DESTROYED WORLD AND THE GUILTY SELF

A Psychoanalytic Study of Culture and Politics

David P. Levine

and

Matthew H. Bowker

PHOENIX
PUBLISHING HOUSE
firing the mind

First published in 2019 by
Phoenix Publishing House Ltd
62 Bucknell Road
Bicester
Oxfordshire OX26 2DS

British Library Cataloguing in Publication Data

A C.I.P. for this book is available from the British Library

ISBN-13: 978-1-912691-13-5

Typeset by vPrompt eServices Pvt Ltd, India

Printed in the United Kingdom

www.firingthemind.com

Contents

About the Authors

David P. Levine is emeritus professor in the Josef Korbel School of International Studies at the University of Denver. He holds a PhD in economics from Yale University and a Certificate in Psychoanalytic Scholarship from the Colorado Center for Psychoanalytic Studies. He has published extensively in the fields of economics, political economy, and psychoanalysis. In the field of psychoanalysis, he has published books on work, creativity, ethics, and politics. His most recent publication is *Dark Fantasy: Regressive Movements and the Search for Meaning in Politics.* He currently lives in Santa Fe, New Mexico.

Matthew H. Bowker is a professor in political science at Medaille College in Buffalo, New York, where he teaches courses in psychoanalytic theory, political philosophy, ethics, and more. He holds degrees from Columbia University and the University of Maryland, College Park and recently (2018) completed a Fulbright grant. He is the author or editor of eleven books—including a volume on the psychoanalysis of *Hikikomori* and severe social withdrawal (forthcoming from Phoenix)—and several dozen articles and chapters on psychoanalysis and politics. He serves as editor (N. America) of the *Journal of Psychosocial Studies*, coeditor of the *Psychoanalytic Political Theory* book series (Routledge), and sits on numerous editorial and advisory boards.

Introduction

In this book, we continue our exploration of cultural and political trends organized around the conviction that the world we live in is a dangerous place to be, that it is dominated by hate and destruction, and that in it our primary task is to survive by carrying on a lifelong struggle against hostile forces (Bowker, 2014; Bowker & Levine, 2018; Levine, 2018). As in our earlier work, our concern is not with the reality of existential threats, but with the conviction that those threats exist, a conviction that, while validated at times by real events, transcends reality-based sources of existential anxiety while fueling and shaping our experience of them.

One form the conviction that we are beset by existential threats takes is fantasies: wish- and fear-invested narratives, images, and dialogues. These fantasies imagine a past, anticipate a future, or describe the present as a time (and place) defined by a violent contest of wills in which the best we can do is struggle to survive against hostile forces. Such fantasies offer evidence that, whether those engaged with them are or are not aware of the fact, there exists at a basic level of their psyches a conviction that the world is a place where survival is always in doubt.

Fantasies exist at two levels of experience: the inner or private world, and external, especially public, space. Public fantasies are distinguished from private by the fact that they are shared. Public fantasy makes the private fantasy seem more real because it appears in public and because it appears there in a more finely drawn and fully conceived form. However unrealistic the public fantasy may be, when it accords with private fantasy, experience of public fantasy affirms the reality of an otherwise subjective experience.

Characters in fantasy represent or embody emotional experiences internalized as self-states. The crystallization of emotional experiences into fantasy characters means that emotions often appear in pure or extreme forms, which are the forms of primitive emotional experience and its continuing presence in adult life. Thus, for example, a fantasy rooted in early emotional experiences of rage or aggression may give rise to fantasy figures who commit acts of violence or cruelty.

That individuals are drawn to such fantasies—and the central fantasy with which we are concerned here is certainly one of extreme emotional states—does not imply that they are driven to act out their fantasy narratives in the world. We should not make the assumption so often made that those who are drawn to extreme narratives must therefore be prone to violent acts, or that mere exposure to violent fantasy causes violence. Doing so misunderstands the meaning and significance of fantasy, while eliding the distinction between fantasy and reality. At the same time, we should not reject the real, if more complex, way in which fantasy narratives do shape what we do in the world outside our fantasy. For instance, violence, whatever its form, is an enactment of fantasy; and our ability to understand violence depends on our ability to sort out the complex relationship between fantasy and reality, or, more precisely, between two kinds of reality: the reality of the inner world (psychic reality) and the reality of the world outside.

The power of public fantasy is a clear indication that something vital in our private lives is shared with others. More than anything else, more than values, more than allegiance to group, community, or nation, it is shared fantasy that binds us together and reveals the meaning of our social connection. Indeed, group affiliations are built out of fantasy and group identification is an enactment of fantasy. The specific meaning of social connection expressed in public fantasy defines the kind of society we live in or wish we lived in. This means that there is a special kind of truth embedded in fantasy so that, even if we are tempted to dismiss fantasy as an escape from reality—which, in an important sense, it is—we should also understand fantasy as an escape in the direction of a different reality, which is the reality of psychic life and of the emotions that are the essential elements there.

The method we employ here to understand social processes and cultural trends is the analysis or interpretation of fantasy. To analyze or interpret fantasy is to explicate the meaning of the activities in which fantasy characters are engaged. Doing so, however, can be problematic. Fantasies are not straightforward tales. Their meanings are rarely what they appear to be, or what the characters in the fantasy narrative tell us they are. Rather, the meaning of fantasy exists on two, often conflicting, levels: (1) what is overtly or explicitly presented in the fantasy narrative, and (2) what is hidden or embedded in it. The analysis of fantasy seeks to identify this second, embedded meaning.

Destruction and Its Aftermath

In this book, we explore the fantasy of the destroyed world. By doing so, we hope to gain insight into something important that lies at the emotional core of our society: a shared state of mind that is, on one level, what being in society is all about. Our primary concern is with the way impulses associated with the destroyed world are expressed or depicted in fantasy narratives that dominate both intrapsychic experience and the public shape that such experience takes. In other words, our interest is in the hold the destroyed world has over us, individually and collectively, which is to say: our fascination with it.

We are also concerned, however, with the way destructive impulses are used to hide more deeply embedded emotional realities of desolation and loss. That is why our attempt to interpret the fantasy of the destroyed world is an effort to understand not merely our preoccupation with destruction, but, more precisely, with destruction's aftermath: a desolate world where living, if possible at all, means little more than surviving. We focus specifically on what might be called the *past tense* of destruction and what it tells us about the quality of the inner world and the nature of its relationship to both private and public realities. For instance, simply noting the emphasis, in destroyed-world fantasies, on the aftermath of destruction offers us a clue to the link between anxiety about present or future existential threats and their hidden psychic meaning: that the anticipated moment of destruction both distracts from and gives expression to the desolation of an inner world where considerable destruction has already occurred.

The destroyed world of fantasy is a world made unfit for human habitation. The things that sustain life – air, food, and water – may have become toxic. The world may have been taken over by aliens intent on eliminating human beings altogether or erasing what is distinctively human in the world. The institutions of government and civil life may have been taken over by malevolent forces. No place is safe. The few who retain their humanity must devote all of their energies to surviving: to discovering water to drink or food they can eat, to fending off the forces bent on their destruction, or to escaping the now uninhabitable world in the hope of finding a new world more conducive to human life. In this last variant of the fantasy, survivors must abandon an Earth no longer capable of supporting human life and seek a new world—a world which, as it turns out, often appears identical to the old world before it was destroyed. In brief, the fantasy of the destroyed world is a fantasy of the radical loss of safe space, the subsequent impossibility of attending to and caring for the self or human spirit, and the desperate search for an environment capable of nurturing body, mind, and soul.

In literary fiction, film, television, and virtual reality entertainment, one readily encounters vivid expressions of destroyed-world fantasy: depictions of extinction-level events and world-ending scenarios, struggles for survival against nonhuman monsters, and, more recently, revisitations of Holocaust-, World War-, and Cold War-narratives, prominently featuring the anxious mood of those living under the threat of genocide, world domination, and/or nuclear annihilation. In popular journalism, *The Washington Post* now presents readers with its (first) official slogan, "Democracy Dies in Darkness," printed just beneath its masthead. More blithely, the cover story of a recent issue of *Popular Mechanics* offers a list of "64 Things to Do Before the World Ends" (2018). If popular media have become engaged with fantasies of destruction, so too have academic literatures, particularly those that advance the ideal of "the death of the subject" and the dawn of the "the post-human" (see Blackman et al., 2008), that valorize self-rending or traumatic experience (e.g. Bataille, 1988; Butler, 2004; Caruth, 1995), that envision the "end of the Anthropocene" (see Jagodzinski, 2018), or that insist that we live "in the end times" (Žižek, 2011).

The prevalence of such expressions of the fantasy of the destruction of the world suggests that this fantasy has a special hold over us, that it has become a subject of shared fascination. The French psychologist Gustave Le Bon (2001, pp. 69–78) describes fascination as a "hypnotic state" in which the fascinated person or group is enveloped by fantasy, appropriates any and all suitable aspects of reality into the fantasy, and, thereby, forfeits contact with reason, reality, "will and discernment," such that "all feelings and thoughts are bent in the direction determined by the hypnotizer" (p. 18).

By speaking of the "appropriation of reality into fantasy," we do not intend to dismiss or diminish the importance of actual destructive forces existing outside our fantasy, nor do we deny that the destruction of the world is a real possibility[1]. But we misunderstand the relationship between destructive fantasies and destructive realities if we treat the fantasy of the destroyed world merely as a fantasy about real acts of destruction. Instead, destructive realities are "appropriated into fantasy" when events involving real-world destruction are experienced in terms of their concordance with personal emotional catastrophes instantiated in the mind as fantasies of destruction.

When this appropriation of the reality of destruction occurs, our understanding of the nature and meaning of real-world threats is distorted, just as our ability to respond to them on a reality-connected basis is compromised. Thus, our concern in this book is not only with the loss of reality connection implied by the appropriation of reality into fantasy, but also with what is expressed when real catastrophes are appropriated and incorporated into fantasy life. In other words, our interest is in what we can learn about the meaning(s) invested in external reality by the power exerted by psychic reality.

While it may seem natural to consider the destroyed-world fantasy primarily in terms of destructive forces in the world, more important in understanding this fantasy is not what is *present* there, but what is *absent*. What is missing from the destroyed world is the good object. For this reason, the best word to describe this world is not "dangerous" but "desolate." In it, we are banished from the presence of the good object, which has been taken away and hidden from us. It has been made inaccessible, sealed behind an impenetrable wall.

Badness, Responsibility, and Guilt

In our fantasy, the good object has gone missing for a reason: namely, because we are "bad" in some essential way. We are bad because we have lost our own good self, which can only exist in the presence of the good object. Before there is badness there is absence. Absence becomes badness when we discover, or, more accurately, create, a causal connection between the two. We discover or create this causal link because, to the extent that we are able to identify the bad self as the entity whose presence is responsible for absence, we also generate hope: the hope that we can retrieve the good object and, once again, become a good self. But this hope is only possible once we have replaced the mere absence of the good object with its destruction.

Destruction, then, becomes the active moment of absence, the moment without which absence can be nothing other than an unalterable (given) fact. In the mental work of fantasy, we transform this fact into the result of an act done by an actor and, therefore, into something that has happened for a reason. We do so because of the conviction that we can fix the things that matter by finding what went wrong, which is to say by creating a relationship in the mind between cause and effect.

At stake in the destroyed-world fantasy, in other words, is the insistence that we live in a destroyed world because someone or something destroyed it, and, therefore that to rectify our predicament requires the assignment of responsibility to destructive forces in our world. In this way, our path out of the destroyed world becomes clear: We must engage those destructive forces in a struggle over hegemony. But, of course, the forces that destroyed our world are fantasy characters we put into it with the hope that we could reverse the effects of destruction by defeating them. These characters were created by us to take responsibility for the absence in our world of an agent capable of caring for us. Preoccupation with destruction, then, becomes preoccupation with responsibility. Our special concern here is with how taking and assigning responsibility protects individuals and groups against the intolerable prospect of the loss of their world, which is also the intolerable knowledge of the fact that their world has already been lost.

The destroyed-world fantasy, then, is an account of where the badness in the world lies and what can be done about it. More specifically, it is a story about the badness of the self. The conviction that the self is bad—along with the psychological, moral, and political consequences entailed by that conviction—has, of course, been a prominent theme in religious and philosophical thought for centuries, as it has become a veritable obsession in contemporary political and ethical theory, where it typically assumes the following form: "To prevent the (bad) self from doing harm to others, the self must be disrupted, disoriented, or incapacitated."

The widespread "revulsion" against the bounded, secure, "Western" self (Hassan, 1987, p. 5) in much late modern and postmodern thought is based on the belief that this self is to blame for the destruction of the world. Indeed, if anything unites the vastly different *oeuvres* of prominent thinkers such as Giorgio Agamben, Georges Bataille, Judith Butler, Cathy Caruth, Jacques Derrida, Michel Foucault, Jacques Lacan, and Emmanuel Levinas, it is the attack on the self-as-subject and the consequent moral imperative that the self be diminished, restricted, or destroyed.

For Georges Bataille, the "father of postmodernism" (Drury, 1994, p. 123), the self must be "lacerated" in *supplice*, a French term that typically refers to torture or torment, but that also alludes to supplication. Torment and supplication ensure that the "appropriative" and exploitative self is broken, and is, in that sense, made amenable to penetration by the Other (1988, pp. 33–61). For Bataille, "the wound that opens up in each participant of the relation permits the flow of material from one to the other" (Faulkner, 2010, p. 106). Indeed, the lacerating of the self creates the wound that "marks the place of loss, the enormity of which tears a hole that opens up being to the communication that unites beings" (Botting & Wilson, 1997, p. 7).

It is of some interest to us that Bataille specifically condemns the individual and collective process he calls rational "appropriation" (1985), a term we have used above to discuss the "appropriation of reality into fantasy." Instead, Bataille defends the appropriation of reality into his fantasy of shared woundedness and mutual (physical and psychic) violation, while rejecting the cognitive processes associated with understanding as debasements of sacred experience, sacrileges to that which must remain overwhelming and unassimilable. Thus, in Bataille, we see the links between (1) the conviction of a bad self, (2) the ethical demand that the self must be lacerated or broken in order *not* to be bad, and (3) the mystifying effect of this laceration or brokenness, which leaves the self confused, lost, and forbidden or unable to think.

Along similar—but less extreme—lines, for Judith Butler, the self must remain "undone" by and before others (2004, p. 23), even if, following Emmanuel Levinas, this undoneness makes the self a "hostage" to the other (see Alford, 2002, p. 29). Like Bataille's tortured, supplicating selves, Butler's self is exhorted to ask, "Who am I?", "What have I become?", and "What is left of me?" (Butler, 2004, p. 30), as "I become inscrutable to myself" (p. 22). That these questions find no answers is understood by Butler as an ethical achievement, since it is our "unknowingness" that makes possible a virtuous community (p. 46).

As in Bataille's and Levinas' thought, for Butler the refusal to close the "open wounds" we inflict on ourselves, as we take on more and more responsibility for harm done to others, becomes the foundation for a public ethic of shared vulnerability where "my own foreignness to myself is, paradoxically, the source of my ethical connection with others." In the "disorientation of grief," which is, again, not just grief at the harm done to others but grief over the infliction of guilt on the self and the ensuing restriction of the self's capacity to be and to act without trepidation, Butler finds an ethical "point of departure" (2004, p. 46): By "remaining exposed to [the] unbearability [of grief]," the self becomes alienated from itself and finds, instead, "a point of identification with suffering itself" (p. 30).

The oriented, bounded, and secure self is, in Butler's (and others') accounts, guilty of imagining itself to be autonomous and is, therefore, flawed and dangerous. "Let's face it," Butler writes, "we're undone by each other. And if we're not, we're missing something." The person who tells a "story" about himself in which his own choices, determinations, and achievements matter more than his "precariousness," his "woundedness" (p. 23), and his self-alienation, is presumed to be lacking an essential quality that would permit him to live harmoniously with others in society. More than that, he is guilty of refusing to take responsibility for the suffering of others, responsibility that is implied in any action grounded in self-determination. By failing to take responsibility, he may force those who suffer to take responsibility for their own suffering. And it may be that, in failing to relieve them of their suffering, he imposes on them—or exposes to them—the source of his own suffering.

To take another influential example, consider Jacques Derrida's claim that any death, even of a single individual, constitutes not just the death of *a* world, the subjective "world" of the deceased. Rather, "each time something dies, it's the end of the world. Not the end of a world, but of the world, of the whole of the world, of the infinite opening of the world" (quoted in Naas, 2015, p. 181, 14n). If we combine Derrida's assertion of radical "singularity" with his critique(s) of mourning, then our subjective orientation to the reality of destruction—even the death of a single individual—can be fairly described as apocalyptic.

Note

1. If it is felt that the term, "possibility," distances us excessively from the havoc being wreaked by "long emergencies" and "converging catastrophes" already underway (Kunstler, 2005), we agree that, in many senses and for many persons, the destruction of the world is a reality. Certainly, the ongoing—but not as yet cataclysmic—degradation of the planet wrought by climate change represents a form of destruction that threatens the capacity of the planet to sustain human life. Similarly, democratic societies find themselves facing the possibility of "erosion," "collapse," or "destruction" from forces within and without, particularly from the activity of extremist groups, from the rise of information warfare, and from nativist and authoritarian movements. The long-standing realities of poverty, hunger, disease, species extinction, and resource scarcity are well known to us, as are terrorism, genocide, and international warfare.

CHAPTER ONE

Godforsaken

In this chapter, we introduce an iconic version of the fantasy of the destroyed world: the myth of the American West. We have chosen this version because it best exemplifies our themes, which, we would argue, are important themes common in fictional narratives of what is referred to as the West, although they are not the only themes we will find highlighted in those narratives. Much of this chapter is devoted to describing the events and characters of the television series, *Godless* (2017), which we will return to throughout the following chapters as an expression of the destroyed-world fantasy and an emblematic and illustrative cultural artifact. Our purpose here is not to consider "what happened" in the Western territories during the second half of the nineteenth century, but to explore the psychic meaning of the West considered not as a historical reality, but as an internal object relation.

The version of the myth of the American West we highlight here is a story of the struggle between the remorseful and the remorseless, between the guilty and the innocent, and between those who are guilty of crimes but feel no guilt, those who are their victims, and those who seek redemption. It is also a story of good fathers and bad fathers, fathers who love and fathers who hate, of innocent women and children, and of women and children who have lost their innocence, who are no longer either women or children. It is a story about gender difference and its roots in the struggle over guilt. And it is a story about the few and the many, the individual and the group.

Finally, and most importantly, the myth with which we are concerned here tells a story about those who have lost their homes, and, with the loss of their homes, have lost a safe space in which to be. Because this story of the search for the lost home is a fantasy, the loss of safe space depicted in it is the loss of safe space in the inner world. The inner world depicted in the fantasy is one that offers no refuge because the most powerful voice in it is one that knows our crimes and calls us to account for them. As we will see in the story of *Godless*, the specific version of the myth of the West with which we are concerned here, it is the voice of Frank Griffin talking to himself, as it is Frank Griffin's mission to punish others for his sins.

The story of the West we are interested in is not "history," unless by "history" we have in mind the echo of archaic object relations in the emotional experience of the here and now. If, then, the Western is, like history, something that happened in the past, it is the psychological and not the historical past: the past that continues to exist in the present as the prism through which relating to others in the world of today is understood and shaped. In sum, it is a story about the self as it was, as it is, and as it might have been.

Myths of the West are frequently stories of being on one's own in the world, stories of self-reliance. But the self-reliance we speak of here is not the self-reliance that nurtures autonomy or the self-made life, what Winnicott refers to as the "doing that expresses being" (1986, p. 39). Rather, it is the self-reliance that is contingent on the individual's ability to defend the self against a world of others bent on its destruction. It is the self-reliance of the walled-off self, kept secure through its own imprisonment (Steiner, 1993). Here, self-reliance becomes equivalent to the capacity to mobilize aggression against powerful, even overwhelming, forces.

It needs to be emphasized that the Western myth treated here is not a description of the inevitable losses implied in the human experience. Rather, it depicts deeply embedded object relations shaped by the intergenerational transmission of early experiences of dislocation. In such fantasies, dislocation becomes a physical matter: Families sever their ties with communities, neighbors, and relatives to move "west." This physical dislocation, because it separates the protagonist of the drama from a safe world, is part of the fantasy of being on one's own in a dangerous place. Above all, the West is a dangerous place.

One prominent version of the story recounts the experience of those who get lost in transition and are fated to wander without hope of finding what they are searching for. Images of the West are often vivid in their emptiness. The landscape is populated by special creatures—snakes, lizards, buzzards, scorpions—well-adapted to its defining qualities, just as it is populated by special kinds of vegetation that thrive without much of what life needs to thrive: cacti, sage, and other shrubs, and the trees that offer little protection from the deadly rays of the sun and little nurturance to those who would attempt to make food out of them.

The story of the western migration comes in many forms, but one that captures the themes centering on remorse, lost parents, and the struggles of young men and of women who are on their own is presented well in *Godless*. Indeed, if there is one word for the mythic landscape of the West, both internal and external, it is "Godforsaken."

Godless

In the opening scene of *Godless*, we follow US Marshal John Cook as he enters the destroyed town of Creede, Colorado. Only burnt-out buildings, dead bodies, and the dust created as a byproduct of destruction remain. In Creede, everything is occluded by dust. Dust accompanies death; it blocks the sun and drains the color out of life.

A lone woman survivor sits on the ground beside a dead man. She is plaintively singing: "He is the power in my soul … Christ is a mystery in my soul." Immediately, we see the irony of the religious theme, the insistence on the presence of God when all available evidence points to God's absence. This world needs God, figured as the (good) Father; and we all suffer in His absence. Those who survive suffer the loss of the power of God in their souls, and, because of this, are no more alive than the dead they mourn.

The marshal looks up and sees a young boy who has been hanged, a symbol of the utter depravity of the gang that destroyed the town, and also an indicator of the real meaning of their act of destruction: to destroy youth and what it represents. As the story unfolds, we discover more and more evidence that the boy at the end of the rope in Creede represents the young Frank Griffin, leader of the gang that destroyed the town. Frank Griffin imagines himself a preacher. He gives sermons and ministers to the sick, while he takes from people what little they have, and often their lives. Although Frank wears a minister's collar, his ministry is one of death and despair. As one of his gang members observes, when Frank says he will save you, he means he will kill you.

Frank and his gang are searching for Roy Goode, Frank's adopted son. Roy Goode spent twelve years as a member of Frank Griffin's gang of thirty men who roam the area of northern New Mexico and southern Colorado robbing mines and engaging in merciless and violent assaults. Roy has turned against Frank. He left the gang but continues to follow and harass it. When Roy rejects the violence of the gang, he must leave and in so doing betray Frank's trust. He cannot do this without guilt. For Roy, love will always be confused with hate. Roy faces the choice of being consumed either by hate or by guilt. He chooses guilt. Seeking punishment as a way of managing his guilt, he turns himself in to the sheriff of La Belle, New Mexico. Yet, as it turns out, breaking with the gang and the violence it represents is no easy matter.

In the aftermath of a showdown with Frank's gang in which both Roy and Frank are injured, Roy approaches Alice Fletcher's house outside La Belle. It is late at night. As is her habit when visited by strangers, and sometimes even by her neighbors, Alice confronts Roy with a rifle and demands that he identify himself. When he fails to do so, she shoots him, then takes him into her home, where the Paiute woman Iyovi, who is the mother of Alice's dead second husband, nurses him back to health.

Alice is twice married, twice widowed. When Alice was seventeen years old she came west to marry her father's business partner, a man named Henry whom she had never met. Henry met her at the train station. On their way home from the station, he wanted to show off his land, "our land, he said." As they were riding, a dark black cloud appeared followed by a six-foot wall of water. "Henry got washed away right in front of me." Alice wandered for eight days in the wrong direction before she was found, first by a gang of men wearing masks who stabbed and raped her, and then by the sheriff of La Belle, who saved her and took her to live with the Paiutes, where she married her second husband. Her second husband was shot in the back in La Belle for no apparent reason other than that he was a Native American. She lives with her son Truckee and Iyovi on her first husband's ranch.

The world of *Godless* is filled with damaged men, women who have lost their husbands, children who have lost their parents, and families who have lost their homes. The primary setting of the series – La Belle – is a mining town that suffered a recent disaster—the collapse of the mine—in which virtually all of the men living there were killed. *Godless*, then, is the story of survivors and the damage done to them by the violence that destroyed their intimate connections.

In episode two, Frank tells the story of his family's trip west. This is the story of the way love and hate have, for him, become inseparable. When he was a young boy, Frank's family travelled west. While travelling, they encountered a group of Mormons masquerading as Native Americans: religious men who raped and killed over 100 people in Frank's party including his whole family. During the carnage, Frank was forced to watch his father killed and his mother raped by the leader of the Mormons, Isaac Hait. "Everyone was left to fester and corrupt in the hot sun."

Everyone was killed except Frank, who was adopted by Hait, who believed that "all things are purified by blood," and that killing gentiles was the path to grace and would lead to salvation. After killing Frank's father and mother, Hait dressed himself in Frank's father's clothes and adopted Frank as his son. This slaughter of his family is the moment of Frank's death, and he has seen it: "When my death comes, I'll be ready, on account I already lived it." Frank, then, represents those who have survived their deaths, those who are living but no longer alive. Frank describes the world in which he is living in the aftermath of his death, the world of the western migration: "God? What God? Look around. Ain't no higher up around here to look after you and your young 'uns. This here is the paradise of the locust, the lizard, the snake. It's the land of the blade and the rifle. It's godless country. All a man can count on is hisself."

While we know how Frank lost his family, we are never told what happened to Roy's parents when Roy and his brother Jim were left alone to travel west to California. We do learn that the brothers, while travelling on their own, were taken in by "Sister" Lucy to live with her and a group of orphans for whom she was caring. While Sister Lucy is in some ways a nun-like figure, she is not a nun, but a prostitute, who, later in the series, finds herself the proprietor of a house of prostitution. After some time spent with Sister Lucy, Jim decides to travel west on his own to seek work, promising to come back for Roy when he has found work in California. Roy appeals to Jim to take him on his trip west, but Jim refuses. After considerable time passes without word from his brother, Roy decides that he has been abandoned and chooses to leave Sister Lucy where Jim had instructed him to remain until he returned. After leaving Sister Lucy, he encounters Frank and is absorbed into Frank's gang as his son.

Roy meets Frank when Frank catches him attempting to steal his horse. Frank approaches Roy who pulls a gun on him. Frank takes the gun away from Roy and asks him: "Tell me, son. You got a pappy?" In response, Roy spits at Frank, to which Frank replies: "Me neither." Frank takes him to the gang's hideout, telling him this is the place he was "born," and it is the place where Roy will be born: "You've got a family now, son … I aim to be your pappy. And a good one. I won't mistreat you. And I won't ever lie to you. Ever. Welcome home, son."

When Frank adopts Roy, Roy is an angry, frightened, injured boy. Like an untamed horse, he is wild and aggressive. He is also alone. His aggression, however, is not primal; he was not born with it, at least not in the form it has taken. Rather, it is aggression wrapped around a bottomless fear linked to abandonment. The original objects of his anger are those on whom he relied but who turned out to be unreliable: his parents and his older brother. Frank seeks to tame Roy as he has tamed his horse. But, Frank's overwhelming hatred and impulse to destroy undermine his bond with Roy, who cannot conflate love with hate in the way they are conflated for Frank.

Taming and Breaking

The horse plays an important role in the story of *Godless* and in much of the mythology of the West. Alice has a herd of horses given to her by the Paiutes, who stole them from Mexicans. These are wild horses that need to be tamed, which means made subject to the will of their owners. Taming horses is not something Alice is able to do. She either does not know how or she lacks the quality of personality needed for it. She asks Roy, who has a special ability to communicate with horses, to stay on and tame her herd. In exchange, he asks her to teach him to read.

The horse represents a primal force, something powerful and wild, and therefore dangerous, but also a force that must be integrated into our lives if we are to survive in the West. Symbolically, then, Alice is asking Roy to tame the wildness that she needs in her life but cannot manage. It can be said that this is why Alice needs a man, why she cannot manage without him. It is also why Truckee needs a father, and why Roy needed Frank. Alice has told Roy that Truckee is afraid to ride, so Roy teaches him. Roy attempts to rescue Truckee from the world of women. "How long you been with these women?" he asks. "Long enough to forget who you are?" On Alice's ranch, Roy seeks to be the good father he lost when he was young, most notably in caring for Alice's horses and offering a father figure for Truckee.

Roy learned to work with horses from Frank, who takes his approach to taming horses from the Greek philosopher Xenophon:

> Taming them makes more sense than breaking them. Rather than hauling and beating the animal he [Xenophon] would use a bit of rope, some gentle restraint, and kindness. Not natural for a horse to be laid down. It makes them amenable but full of fear. Makes it hard for him to do what he wants to do, which is bolt. So, he's got to trust you. Despite what some men think, it's not just about showing him who's boss. It's about showing him that that you're the one who's going to feed him and water him. You're the one who's going to take care of him. About showing him he can trust you always and forever. Family's everything, son. Without family, we're lost. Do you trust me, son? 'Cause I ain't your brother. I will never leave you. Not ever.

The godless world is a world defined by the distinction between taming and breaking. You can force cooperation by using violence to coerce the horse to bend to your will. Or, you can use care and kindness to create a bond of affection. Where there is a bond of affection, cooperation depends not on the destruction of the horse's will—the wildness in it—but on the horse's willing cooperation. Where the bond of affection is not formed, subjecting the horse to the force of an overpowering will means destroying its spirit, in other words: soul-death. When the soul dies, the result is an endless wandering in the wilderness, a hopeless longing, a bottomless rage.

In the narrative, taming the wild horse is a metaphor for the relationship through which the child gains control of emotions and impulses, control needed to be an adult in an adult world. But, not only is this control needed for adult living, it is also needed for self-determination. Self-determination does not mean acting on impulse, but refers to the translation of the individual's true self, spirit, or vitality into a concrete, particular identity expressive of it. In particular, there can be no self-determination where the individual is unable to mobilize aggression in defense of the self-boundary. This mobilization of aggression in service of the separate self is possible only where the individual has developed the capacity to contain aggression. Containing aggression requires that we have access to our aggression, so that we can put it in service of the defense of the self-boundary, while also limiting its use to that purpose, rather than finding in aggression the power to attack the self-in-other.

Our ability to contain, access, and limit aggression can only develop where our aggression is not experienced as a threat to the connections with others on whom we depend. So far as aggression is equated with the impulse and power to destroy the self-in-other, and therefore the differences that establish separate selves, its repression will be a precondition for relating, and therefore for participating in systems of relating. So far as this equation is established as a primary psychic reality, the separation of persons, which is the condition for and the result of the active presence of the self, must also be experienced as an attack on the self. Then, the individual who aspires to self-determination finds him- or herself in a double bind. The solution, so far as it can be considered a solution, is to drive the self underground, to hide it in a way that assures it will not be present either as a reality of the inner world or in the world outside.

In *Godless*, the modalities of the transition to adulthood are represented in two ways of managing a horse, one of which involves the violent subjection of the animal to the will of its owner. The other involves establishing a bond of love and with it creating the desire to accept limits as an aspect of a relationship with a good object and of the care provided by it. Whether the horse will be tamed or broken depends on the relation of the primitive self to the paternal object internalization of which is the process of making the self the moving force in shaping identity. It should be emphasized here that, just as the maternal object need not be female, so the paternal object need not be male.

Alice needs Roy to tame, but not break, the horse inside. In other words, she needs a paternal object she can call on to manage her aggression and secure her self-determination. She needs the safe connection with her own wild self that Roy provides for her, but it must be kept outside where it is not directly associated with her. Throughout the series, Alice's demeanor is one of sadness mixed with determination. She is strong in the way those who survive in the West must be strong: They must have the strength to survive their own death, which she did. Her strength, therefore, depends on her having lost her ability to make contact with her vital center. Through Roy, she hopes she might have found a conduit back to it.

Roy, for his part, needs Alice to teach him to read and write. Learning to read is important because it will enable Roy to read a message from his brother that proves he has not abandoned Roy and tells him that he wants Roy to join him in California. Earlier, when Roy leaves his home with Sister Lucy, Lucy gives him this letter and says, “Maybe you’ll learn to read.” This flashback appears immediately after a scene in which Roy and Alice are reading lost letters Roy found in a mail bag in a river, letters written to husbands by the wives they left behind when travelling west. These letters, and the messages in them, will never be received, and, when they are not, their absence will provoke intense feelings of loss. If Roy can learn to read, he can read the lost letter from his brother, which means he will be able reestablish the connection with his lost brother and, therefore, will be able to leave the world of the living dead, the world of endless wandering in a dangerous place. For Roy, then, the connection with Alice is a conduit back to his lost family. If the connection is broken – if the mail is not read—what is wild within becomes destructive. It becomes destructive because disconnection means the loss of a loved object and, of equal importance, a space where love predominates. Disconnection with loved ones in the world outside, then, represents the loss of the benign environment of the inner world.

Fathers and Sons

For the child, soul-death produces the kind of love that is also a form of hate, a form of aggression made all the more intense by its repression. This shared soul-death, and the violence born of it, is the bond that Frank expects to share with Roy. The result of the forming of this bond is the outlaw gang, to be discussed in more detail below. In the filmic and literary genre of the Western, evil (greed and hate) resides in gangs of men who are opposed by individual men (the sheriff, the marshal, and eventually Roy). The odds are not good. But, even though Frank is driven to mold his relationship with Roy into this pattern, he is also committed to taming rather than breaking the horse inside Roy. This means that Frank is no simple incarnation of hate, violence, and evil, but the site of the struggle between the residue of the boy Frank was before he lost his parents and the man he became after they were taken from him.

Yet, Frank differs from Roy. While Frank lost his parents in a brutal assault, and assumes that Roy, having lost his parents, must be like him, it turns out that this is not the case. The little direct information we have comes from a brief account of his attempt to separate from Frank: “When I left Frank, I started having crazy thoughts. I could not leave him alone. I started stealing from him, harassing him.” But, neither was Roy able to kill Frank, "at least not until I heard what he did in Creede on account of me." Roy could not "leave" Frank because, to escape Frank, he would have to escape the part of himself attached to, or represented by, Frank. To do this, he felt that he would have either to kill Frank or be killed by him. Because he could not kill the Frank in his mind, he had to kill the Frank outside and hope that this would produce the same result. But, how do you kill an object in the mind? And how do you cope with the guilt you feel for killing your father; indeed, how do you cope with the guilt you feel for the impulse within you to do so?

During Frank's search for Roy, he makes it clear that he will destroy anyone who offers Roy refuge. He will not just kill those who come to Roy's aid, he will destroy the whole town that harbors him and all the people in it. Early in the series, Frank and his gang interrupt a church service. The parishioners are singing "Nearer My God to Thee." Frank rides his horse up to the pulpit and offers his own sermon at the end of which he tells the parishioners: "You all know I don't ever want to come back here and burn this house of the Lord down to the ground. So, let's all bow our heads and pray that Roy Goode don't never show up here. But that if he does, none of you well-meaning souls take him in unless you want to suffer like our Lord Jesus Christ. Amen."

From what we learn about Roy, we can surmise, although we do not know, that his violent impulse directed toward his father did not originate with his experience with Frank, but earlier, when he lost his father and was abandoned by his older brother. To the extent that Roy loved both his father and his older brother, and we have good reason to believe that he did, his violent impulse directed at them would provoke guilt at least commensurate with it. Here, we need to bear in mind that, psychologically, especially for a child, to lose a parent is to be abandoned by that parent even if, considered from an adult standpoint, the parent in no way willed or caused the loss to occur. In the child's mind, and for the adult dominated by more primitive modes of thought, the will of the all-powerful figure of the parent is always the causal factor.

The assumption that Roy loved the father he lost gains support from a scene in a graveyard. In this scene, Roy is dragging a coffin to a cemetery, where he digs up a grave, removes the clothes from the dead man buried there, puts on the dead man's clothes, places the dead man into the coffin, and buries the coffin in the grave. Later, we find out that the grave was his father's, and dressing in the clothes of the dead was a way of connecting himself with his lost father. Roy recalled his father wearing those clothes and he put them on in order to join him.

Continuing the theme of dressing himself in the clothes of the dead, Roy dresses in the clothes that belonged to Alice's dead second husband. All of this underscores Roy's wish to be dead, as that is the only path he has, or can imagine, to reuniting with his father. The wish to be reunited with his father in death is coupled with his emotional self-destruction in the form of intense guilt. This is guilt born of the destructive impulses directed at those he loves who have abandoned him. After all, we are aware, from Roy's participation as a gang member for ten years, how intense is Roy's anger and destructive impulse.

We also know that Frank, for all his considerable hatred, in his way loved Roy and was dedicated to being the father Roy never had, which is to say the father that would never, ever abandon him. He would treat Roy as he treated a wild horse, with love rather than violence. Here, as with Roy's lost father, parental love is inseparable from death since, as we have seen, Frank's death occurred before he met Roy, so bonding with Frank meant embracing the dead. And, not betraying Frank meant sharing his hate and participating in his acts of destruction, which are reenactments of his death.

The fantasy of killing Frank, not to mention the reality of doing so, could not be put to rest because of the love Roy has for Frank. Because of this, Roy's need to kill Frank was offset by, one might say expressed as, a need to have Frank kill him. For Frank to kill Roy would be for Frank to relieve Roy of his guilt. On this level, Roy's harassment of Frank was an effort to provoke Frank to kill him, and his need for Frank to kill him bound the two together even as it struggled against Roy's need to live, which he could only do if he could purge Frank from his soul, which is to say kill him.

The climactic scenes of the series feature a violent confrontation in which the women of La Belle become men in order to defend their town against Frank's gang, leaving a handful of survivors, and a showdown between Frank and Roy in which Roy is injured and Frank is killed. There is loss (so many dead), survivor guilt for those who did not die, and also loss of innocence (the women have killed and destroyed). Father attempts to kill son; son kills father. Remaining at the end of the violent battle are many children that were in hiding during the gunfight. They are twice orphaned and survivors of destroyed homes, destined to live in a destroyed world.

There is a funeral scene in which the long-awaited preacher (throughout the series his arrival has been anticipated by some, doubted by others) asks the survivors in La Belle to "love what death has touched," which can be said to be the theme of the whole drama. God, in the form of the preacher, has arrived too late. In the final scenes, Roy travels to California to join his brother. In the last moment of the drama, a moment that undermines its tragic vision, we see Roy looking out over the Pacific Ocean poised to begin a new life away from and free from the terms of the Western fantasy, as if one could escape the destroyed inner world simply by moving away from its geographic location in the world outside.

The Gang

Although he had lost his parents, Roy had a strong relationship with his brother that reinforced his identification with good internal objects. This relationship was, however, disrupted when his brother set off for California in search of work, leaving Roy with Sister Lucy. Sister Lucy also offered a good object with whom Roy could develop a relationship, but that relationship was not sufficient to replace the connection with his brother, who, in turn, had replaced his parents. Roy was disappointed by being left behind but reassured by his brother's promise to return. Still, as time passed, Roy's trust in his brother's promise weakened until the point was reached at which he lost hope that his brother would return, and, as a result, the valence of the object represented by him shifted from good to bad. At this point, intense anger directed toward his brother took over. He left Sister Lucy and eventually formed an attachment to Frank Griffin based on Frank's offer of an opportunity for Roy to act out his considerable aggression through gang violence. Even so, it cannot be said that Frank had nothing positive to offer, as exemplified most notably in the way Frank taught Roy to work with horses. This also drew Roy to Frank and assured that his time in the gang would be a time of internal struggle over the valence of the internal objects with which he would be most powerfully identified.

This struggle took a particular form having to do with the way Roy's intensified aggression directed toward his good objects, as represented especially by his brother, made his inner world a dangerous place for those objects to be, just as it made any identification with them risky because his experience of connection with them was one in which that connection always led to loss and suffering. The gang offered a suitable system for solving this problem by assuring, that, within it, there would be rapid and severe punishment for any identification with the good objects, which would always be equated with weakness. In other words, the gang would represent and reinforce the defense against contact with the self. After all, what makes an object good is the experience of safety in being connected to your self when connected to the object.

Psychologically, the gang is the fantasized solution to the problem of the abandoned child. The "new family" Frank offered Roy was one in which all the members were driven by destructive impulses and in whose company not only would Roy be able to act out his aggression, he would also be assured that his internal good object relationships would be aggressively repressed. The guilt Roy felt for the destructive acts of his gang, or new family, indicated, however, the continuing strength of his internal good objects built up through internalization of his relationships with his brother, Sister Lucy, and his parents.

By contrast, for Frank, intense violence dominated the experience of parental loss, while the new object he found to replace his parents was also the source of violence. As a result, he was left without hope for reunion with his good objects. What had been an affectionate connection with his parents was now replaced by the impulse to destroy innocence as the imagined solution to the vulnerability and dependence implied in it. The idea that you could only save people by killing them expressed the dilemma in which he found himself: You can only keep the vital center and vulnerable core secure by ruthlessly attacking it to assure that its presence will never be known or felt, as that would only invite harm. The presence of innocence invites destruction. This is the central emotional theme of the gang in which the "destructive part of the self … tyrannizes the dependent needy part" (Steiner, 1993, p. 51).

For Frank, the gang represents the ever-present violence needed to keep the vital self walled off. The members of the gang represent the destructive forces in the psyche established there to prevent any connection with the vulnerable self, which is experienced as the cause of suffering because it invites aggression. Internalization of his new father, Isaac Hait, took the form of an identification with the aggressor, a process of the formation in Frank's psyche of a menacing force capable of assuring that no contact with the true self would ever be made. This development assured the eclipse of any internalized good object relationship and, therefore, the loss of the capacity for love. Without love there can be no guilt, so this development also assured that there would be no remorse for any harm done to others. It should not be surprising, then, to discover that Frank came to define love as the union of the hateful.

Taken as a whole, the drama depicts the struggle between two powerful forces within the psyche, one tied to the hope for the return of the lost good object, one tied to the absence of any such hope. In the drama, this struggle is depicted as a life and death conflict in which only one force can survive. And, understood as a fantasy, this is, indeed, a depiction of the struggle between those forces allied with psychic life and those allied with psychic death.

In this struggle, the gang is a psychic organization whose purpose is to build a fortress of aggression against the self as the only means available for protecting it from a hostile world. At the same time, the gang is the presence in the inner world from which the self must be protected. Internally, the true self is "surrounded by, and submits to, malevolent feral infant gangs as immediate guardians of the internal fortresses of psychic retreats" (Mojovic, 2017, p. 148; on psychic retreats, see Steiner, 1993).

Because of the power of aggression in the (inner) world, survival requires access to a force multiplier, which appears in the gang first as strength in numbers and second as the supernatural powers of the gang leader. The multitude of members also serves to hide the individual in a mass by enforcing discipline in the form of adherence to the rule that any meaningful expression of separate being or unique presence will be suppressed. At the same time, the multiplication of members represents the fragmentation of the inner world attendant upon the loss of the self, which is the loss of the integrating power within the personality. Fragmentation means that what might otherwise be an integrated whole is experienced as a chaos of emotions, internal object relations, and out-of-control impulses each demanding to be fed with its characteristic object be that money, sex, or violence.

In many myths and narratives of the West, we find the depiction of an internal struggle in which guilt is mobilized to defend the self against destruction, a struggle in which guilt is the only available refuge in what would otherwise be a destroyed world. This is also a struggle to achieve or preserve psychic integration depicted as the return of the good object, or, at the end of the drama, the successful completion of a journey to refind the good object (Roy's brother) in the promised land (California). The more intense the aggression directed at the good objects, aggression personified here by Frank and his gang, the more remote the possibility of recourse to guilt as a defense against the transformation of the inner world into a destroyed or godless place. The outlaw gang is the obstacle preventing reunification with the lost good object. Their lawlessness represents the absence of a sufficiently powerful integrating force in the psyche. Law and order, defined in the space of guilt and punishment, no matter how primitive and violent they may be, are the only real barriers against the psychic disintegration and despair attendant upon loss of contact with the self. Thus, the lawman stands, often alone, against the forces of chaos.

But, as it turns out, for Roy, guilt is a false solution to the problem premised on a faulty interpretation. Turning himself in to the sheriff to be hanged will solve his problem in exactly the way modelled for him by Frank: he will save himself by killing himself. The solution is not killing himself or killing Frank, even though that is what he does, but leaving the destroyed world behind and reuniting with his brother in California (just as the solution for Alice is to sell her dead husband's ranch and leave La Belle). In other words, the solution is not a life of doing penance for your sins or purifying your inner world of any presence of destructive impulses there, but finding your way out of the destroyed world, which is a world where repair is a Sisyphean task.

The Town and the Rule of Law

As the story moves towards its inevitable confrontation in La Belle, the audience cannot but wish for, and expect, the appearance of the one man who can defeat the gang: Roy Goode. But Roy, knowing that Frank is searching for him and that Frank will destroy anything and everything in his path, or that he imagines lies in his path, especially by harboring Roy, leaves town so that the people there will not become the victims of Frank's bottomless desire for destruction. In this expectation, Roy is wrong. Roy believes that he is the target of Frank's wrath, and, in this, he is correct, but only up to a point. Roy seems to believe that he is responsible for Frank's destructive rampage, when he was only a container, symbol, or incarnation for the object of Frank's rage. That object is the town itself, which is the place in which it is safe to be.

The Western town embodies a fantasy of civil society in its primitive or nascent state. As a fantasy, it depicts the essential element of civil society, which is a system of relations among people who are not familiar to us – not family members. These people, who exist outside our boundaries, are known primarily in their formal roles – shopkeeper, sheriff, innkeeper, banker – so their internal presence means we have formed a template for relating formally rather than on the basis of what is unique and particular about ourselves. By contrast, the gang fantasy not only excludes relations of this kind, it is hostile to them and seeks their destruction.

Envy plays an important role in fostering the hostility of the gang toward the town. In the town, the gang member sees settled lives, lives that are not dominated by relentless attacks on the self, but that facilitate contact with it to the extent that private space is protected. In other words, the town represents safe space for a private life, something noticeably absent in the gang. Indeed, on one level, the gang is all about the destruction of private space for its members. This suggests that one important feature of the internal gang is that the characters in it are unable to use private space and even feel threatened by it. Private space is inner space and the use of private space means turning inward, which is something the gang member cannot do.

Law in the fantasy world protects inner space, just as, in the space outside the fantasy, law protects the integrity of the individual: his or her life and property, where property is the means used by the individual or family to demarcate private space. The state of lawlessness indicates the absence of safe space whether we are considering inner space or the world outside. Law protects safe space by defending the world against the destructive power of the bad objects. In this, law embodies the presence of a good object powerful enough to contain the destructive impulse represented in the bad. In this, law defends order against chaos.

In the primitive mind, order refers to the correspondence between being good and being cared for, which develops into the correspondence between reward and punishment, which sets the foundation for the whole idea of fairness as getting what is due to you or what you deserve. This correspondence is the original form of causation, and therefore reason. In this sense, the rule of law is the rule of reason, whereas, outside the law, reward and punishment are allocated not for reasons but arbitrarily, according to power and will.

Lawlessness begins when the parents "die" before the children are able to care for themselves. When this happens, the incipient integration of the inner world is disrupted, and the children reconstruct the inner world as a gang of destructive emotions represented as internal objects that pose a threat to the true self. This chaotic and dangerous world of conflicting emotions is, then, projected outside so that the external, or "real," world is experienced as an enactment of the inner drama. The external world made dangerous by the absence of the parent in it is reconceived as a struggle between forces representing lawlessness and forces representing the power of the law to control emotion in the absence of any power in the external world capable of doing so (the parent). Then, the child may attempt to create or join a gang in the world outside (make the fantasy real) as a defense against the projection there of harsh internal objects and the intense emotions they represent.

The problem lies in the way abandonment fosters the creation of a harsh internal object to impose order on the chaos of emotional life not conceived as the rule of law but as forceful imposition of will, as is the case in the use of shame to control self-expression (see Chapter Five). The harshness of the internal objects active in this struggle derives in part from the intensity of the fear and aggression provoked by the loss of the parent, and in part from the incomplete process of integration of good and bad, which remains, at the time the parent is lost, a project yet to be finished.

The world outside is, then, experienced as populated by the incarnations of fantasy objects representing poorly integrated emotions in constant war with one another: incarnations, for example, of greed, envy, hate, love, and guilt, all organized around reenactment of the loss of love's object and the hope for its return. Love becomes deeply interpenetrated with hate, intimacy with violation; walls are created to defend against feelings of love and dependence. Hate for the lost object turns the representatives of that object in the mind into harsh and assaultive figures: The mother becomes the prostitute who seduces men, love becomes the violent act of rape that represents vengeance against the mother who is no longer available, paternal love is represented by a fire and brimstone preacher who saves you by killing you.

It needs to be emphasized that central to the fantasy depicted in *Godless* is the chaos resulting from the disintegration of civilization. Above all else, this drama is the expression of the lost power of the inner world to organize experience, to instantiate reason there: to assert direction, purpose, or meaning. The fantasy of the West is a fantasy about the imposition of order, especially in the sense of the assignment of reason and responsibility. This is a fantasy about a lawless world and the heroic image of a "lawman" capable of imposing order there.

In the specific version we find in *Godless*, the lawmen were unable to do their job. A US marshal featured early in the series is killed by Frank. The sheriff who pursues Frank is going blind, and, in any case, has little chance of prevailing against Frank's gang of thirty violent men. The sheriff's attempt to enlist the US Army in defense of the town fails. This is another way to understand the meaning of the title: The world of *Godless* is a world with neither law nor any agent with the capacity to enforce the law. It is the inner world of the child who has lost his parent, of the child who must create fantasy figures organized around existential threats and the gaining of superhuman powers to counter them in order to compensate for his or her loss.

In the typical version of the fantasy of the West, the outlaw gang cannot be allowed to triumph. This is fantasy after all, and it matters little whether the result of the climactic confrontation seems plausible when what matters is that mothers can withstand the father's destructive force. But there is also a dark fantasy featuring the triumph of figures representing dark emotions. In this fantasy, we identify not only with Roy, but with Frank, not only with Alice, but with the gang of women who remain after the loss of their husbands in the mining disaster, not only with law and order, but with chaos and destruction.

CHAPTER TWO

Being Wrong

How the Fantasy Takes Shape

To understand the meaning and impact of the fantasy of the destroyed world, we must first consider how this fantasy takes shape in the mind. To do so, consider a child who awakens one day, alone, in a new and unfamiliar world. What makes this world unfamiliar to the child is the fact that he is alone in it. And he is alone not because there are no people there, but because he feels no connections with them; they are strangers to him. These strangers look like people he knows; but they are not. For the child, these people are not the people he knows because they do not make him feel safe. So, if they look like the people he knows, they have changed in some unaccountable way. They are not who they appear to be. The new world does not make sense to the child because, for him, "making sense" means fitting relationships into the template set in place in the old world, a safe world, he used to inhabit[1].

Fitting into the old-world way of relating is inseparably bound up with care. The people in the old world cared about, attended to, and loved the child; their presence in the world meant that the child mattered because he mattered to them. In their absence, the child is unable to hold onto the idea that he matters. That he matters cannot, for the child, be separated from attentiveness to his emotional existence. In other words, he knows that his existence matters because it elicits a response from others that confirms that it does. By contrast, the new world is marked by its unresponsiveness.

This unresponsiveness means that nothing less than the child's emotional existence, which is to say his presence in the world as a center of emotional experience, is cast into doubt. The experience of the loss of the feeling that he matters now becomes a permanent part of the child's inner world. There, it takes the form of a sense of uncertainty, futility, inner deadness, and existential anxiety.

If the child does not matter, then nothing does. If his expressions of emotion do not elicit the needed responses, then he has no power to create meaning in the world. The child may reasonably experience his situation as a defect in the world in which he finds himself. For him, there is something fundamentally wrong there. But he also experiences the absence of a responsive presence as a defect in himself. It indicates his inability to provoke the responses that confirm his significance to others, which then indicates that he has no significance, that there is something missing not in his world but in himself.

This interpretation has everything to do with what awakening in the new world means to the child. The moment of awakening is the moment the child discovers his separate existence, the moment he loses the seamless unity with his environment, which guaranteed responsiveness and attentiveness to his presence. In other words, the moment of awakening is the moment the child achieves self-awareness, or the separation of the world into self and other. But, if the new world is too abruptly imposed or too different from the old world, achieving self-awareness is linked to the evacuation of meaning from the self and the world. This loss of meaning is the essence of the destroyed world.

If the people the child finds in his new world are unlike—in the most important ways—those he knew in the old world, then who are they, or, more specifically, who are they to him? To answer this question, we must understand something about how the child knows the people in his world and what it means to know them. In simple terms, for the child, knowing people means knowing the state of mind he has when those people are present and available to him. In other words, he knows people by the emotions attached to or experienced in their presence. It can even be said that, for the child, people represent, or incarnate, emotional states. Put another way, persons are containers of emotion. Thought about in this way, the strangers who populate the new world are known by the self-states their presence arouses. This means that they are known by that most salient quality that links them to the people in the old world: the people of the new world are known by, or represent, the absence of the old-world people and, therefore, the absence of the self-states associated with the presence of the people he knew.

The people in the new world are the negation of the people the child formerly knew, just as they negate the emotions formerly experienced in the presence of the people of the old world. They represent the object in whose presence he ceases to exist rather than the object in whose presence he comes into existence. In light of this absence, and owing to the fact that the figures in the new world represent the child's emotional states, the child may find that the people in the new world represent an intensification of need and a link between intensified need and aggression—aggressive impulses rooted in the child's response to his deprivation. These figures may represent the child's longing for the old-world figures, who now exist only in a remembered past and a wished-for future. At the same time, the new-world figures may represent the child's envy for the person he once was but is no longer: the object of—and the object worthy of—care and attention.

By knowing the people of his new world in this way—that is, by knowing them as containers for his own emotional states—the child makes presence out of absence; he populates his new world in a way consistent with the way of knowing he used in the old world. There are now, in the world, tangible representations of absence, which, in one sense, has become something positive. The child has made the transition from the absence of familiar objects to their negation. This movement is assured by two closely linked aspects of the child's situation: (1) his awakening to his subjectivity or vital presence as a causal factor in the world, and (2) the aggression provoked by the fear, even terror, he feels as a consequence of being without the objects that represent for him feelings of safety, being cared about, and, in this way, existing in the world.

To the extent that his psychic existence is contingent on the presence of a responsive environment, an environment in which he matters, being in the new world of strangers frightens the child because he still depends on those who know him to know that he exists; he cannot sustain himself without them. To try to manage his anxiety, he mobilizes the only means he has available to protect himself in a dangerous world: aggression. Mobilization of aggression fills the world of absence in which the child finds himself. It injects emotion, and therefore meaning, into that world. Specifically, it attaches meaning to the absences personified by the strangers in the new world: They are "known" to pose a threat to him because they are identified with his aggressive state.

Aggression can be considered the active aspect of absence because it makes absence the result of an act or acts that negate, or destroy, presence (in this case the presence of the old world and the relationships of which it consisted). It is easy, then, to arrive at the conclusion, as we all have at one time or another, that negating (destroying) the object that represents absence will create presence. And this conclusion is not entirely mistaken, at least not in the (limited) sense in which acting negates the absence of subjectivity by making the source of aggression (the self) the causal factor in the world. In other words, aggression may function as an assertion of presence.

Unfortunately, since the child's aggression, in this context, has been mobilized in response to absence with the aim of imposing his presence, the child ends up becoming both the victim of and the cause of the loss of his world. That is, when he solves the problem of absence by identifying himself with an aggressive self, he makes himself the cause of his exile to the new, dangerous world. If the destructive figures in the new world are containers for the child's aggression and are scripted to be the cause of the destruction of the old world, then it is really the child's aggression that destroyed the old world and created the new. In other words, to make sense of the disjunction between the old world and the new, the child must pay the price of the loss of innocence.

All or virtually all children wake up to a state of self-awareness; and, in so far as they do, all or virtually all children are required at some point to manage the transition to a world populated by strangers. It is not our intention to assert that all children awaken to self-awareness in identical ways, nor to imply that all confront or manage anxiety about living in the new world by identical means. It matters to what degree the transition is experienced as the abrupt disappearance of the original connection with the parents, or a gradual maturation toward independence. In other words, it matters if children are cast into the new world because their parents have become, to one degree or another, strangers to them.

The loss of parents to illness, death, the breakup of the family, and other less obvious but no less significant forms of parental change, absence, or withdrawal—all may promote fantasies of waking up a stranger in a strange land, even if that land does not appear to be different. This waking up entails a radical disjunction between appearance (what is familiar) and reality (what has become strange), that challenges and often overwhelms the child's capacity to make sense of himself and his world. The formation of fantasies responds to this challenge by allowing the child to make sense of his otherwise incomprehensible situation. But the formation of fantasies also makes the experience of absence (shaped by fantasy) a constitutive aspect of the experience of living in the world.

We are familiar with fantasies of estrangement and desolation as they appear in the world of adolescence and adulthood, and as they have come to dominate cultural expressions of psychic reality. As we noted in the Introduction, they may take on a variety of cultural forms organized around the idea of a world made uninhabitable through natural or man-made disaster, a post-apocalyptic dystopia in which the strange new world of the child's experience is appropriated into a fantasy of destruction and inevitable destructiveness that explains how the old world was lost and the new world brought into being in its place.

Seeking Reasons

Waking up in the new world is an event without reason. The new world is not created, or, at least, its creation is not witnessed or known directly; it is simply there; it appears out of nowhere; it is all absence, no presence. To the extent that the new world remains a brute, inexplicable, given fact, the child's anxiety has no limit and his psychic life is over. To protect himself against the intolerable prospect of the immovable facticity of the new world in which he finds himself, he creates, in imagination, the forces that destroyed the old world. If the child can summon or discover in the new world agents responsible for his emotionally destructive experience, then his situation can be made comprehensible to him and he may hold out hope of managing life in, if not necessarily thriving in, his new world. And yet, in the narrative he develops to make sense of his world, the child creates figures who represent not only the loss of presence and care but the denial of reason.

For the child, the idea that reason rules the world is not a philosophical conceit but a desperately important conviction linked to his emotional survival. The figures he creates to attack reason embody the child's own doubt that there is reason in the world, along with his fear that believing in reason will only foster false hope, leaving him vulnerable to further disappointment and loss. The challenge for the child, then, is to hold onto the conviction that reason rules the world by defeating the sinister figures—figures he created—that represent reason's negation. Although the child is now locked in a lifelong struggle against destructive forces, it is, at least, a meaningful struggle, a struggle waged to hold onto the idea that there is reason, and therefore the possibility of meaning and subjectivity in the world. The alternative, to fail in this struggle, is to be vanquished by the irrational, to be overwhelmed by figures bent on destroying reason and meaning and, with them, the child's inner life.

Just as the child moves himself, via imagination, from a world of absence to a world of negation, the child also moves himself, via imagination, from a desolate and empty world without agency or reason to a world under siege by the forces of destruction all around him. Of course, these agents are really containers for the child's own aggression, mobilized in response to his own abandonment and, thus, he can never defeat them absolutely. But if the destructive figures in the new world are containers for aggression and are scripted to be the cause of the destruction of the old world, then it is his aggression that destroyed the old world and created the new. In other words, the loss of innocence is the price he pays for making sense of the disjunction between the old world and the new.

What we hope to have emphasized in this discussion of the creation of agency and the attribution of responsibility is that the new world is not only characterized by a contest of good versus evil—although it is typically depicted in this way, for reasons which we will discuss in the coming chapters—but, at a deeper level, by a struggle over *reason*, which is to say over whether the predicament in which the child finds himself has come about for a reason or for no reason at all.

The child's narrative about his world and his life can have neither meaning nor purpose if reason has no place in it. There can only be meaning and purpose if the land in which he awakens is the way it is not because the destructive figures in his fantasy destroyed the old world to create the new, but because they were created to populate an empty land. In other words, it is not aggression and destruction that define the new world, as much as that seems to be the case, but absence as that is represented in an empty and barren landscape. In the language of the fantasy presented in Chapter One, what defines the new world is God's absence from it.

But, just as the child has understood his new world through a narrative about destructive forces personified as characters in the drama of his new life, he has also scripted himself into his story. The story, after all, is his story. It is the story of his life, and he is the central character in it.

It could be said, of course, that he is *all* the characters in the narrative. The characters in the story represent the child's accountability for his own death, just as they represent his struggle against fear and the use of aggression to solve the dilemma presented by the otherwise obdurate facts of his new existence. Put only slightly differently, the child's story about the destroyed world is really the story of his aggression, his fear, his hope for the return of the good object, or in the language used in the following chapters, his hope for God's return.

But, among the characters that populate his narrative, one has a special place. There is one with whom he seeks to identify more than any other, one that represents the child who wakes up in the new world and faces life in it with hope and fear: the protagonist of the story. His identification with the protagonist of the story represents an insistence on the presence of subjectivity or agency in the world: that the world is not the way it is because of the irreducible fact of the presence of a death instinct or because it is programmed into his nature as part of species or gender; it is the way it is because of the presence of subjectivity in it.

The challenge of the new world is one of discovering reason and subjectivity in order to assign responsibility for destruction and in order to defend against the futility of inhabiting a meaningless, irrational world. Since, as we have discussed above, the quest for reason and subjectivity entails the search for responsibility, inevitably the question of guilt arises. If the child has been abandoned, who has abandoned him? Why has he been abandoned? Is he deserving of abandonment? Is it in the child's power to overcome or repair the desolation he now faces? Does he do so by accepting guilt or by finding it in others? Guilt, as we hope to show in the following section, expresses, in part, the wish for a reason potent enough to rescue the child from the meaninglessness and chaos of the destroyed world.

Basic Fault

Guilt plays a central role in the drama scripted originally by the child who awakens in a new and unfriendly world. But the guilt that plays a role in the drama is not always what it seems. We can see how this might be the case if we bear in mind that taking responsibility for the destruction of the old world is less a realization that the child did, in fact, destroy it, and more an attempt to hold onto his subjectivity in a new world where subjectivity is at risk. We can begin to understand the complexity of guilt if we consider more closely the challenge of making sense of the new world. For the child, and for the adult he will become, this matter of making sense appears most notably as the matter of figuring out the world, or "getting it right" and doing "the right things."

The need to "get it right" and the concomitant fear that we will "get it wrong" are powerful motivating forces in shaping what we do and how we relate to others, particularly if this need, along with the need to "do something right," come to be defined on a moral plane. If they do, then our moral standing—our goodness or badness—is put at risk when we strive to understand the world and when we try to decide what to do in it. Nevertheless, the struggle to get things right and to avoid getting them wrong can provoke significant anxiety even when no obvious issue of moral standing is involved. This suggests that doing things incorrectly and doing wrong to others, while both important in themselves, can also be important for what they imply about right and wrong in a more general sense that may not implicate our identification with the good. To grasp the complexity of the role played by guilt, then, we must begin not with guilt, but with the underlying issues of "being right" and "being wrong."

The moral construction of right and wrong can be used to substitute for, and prevent awareness of, a more basic or underlying concern. No matter how emotionally charged the moral construction, and no matter how substantial the suffering associated with moral failure, there is a deeper kind of suffering the prospect of which can sponsor a flight into the moral world of guilt, reparation, punishment, and justice, along with the suffering associated with being there. This flight into morality has a uniquely powerful influence on the form and intensity of social and political conflict in societies where the matter of personal responsibility plays a prominent role. Indeed, the rhetoric of politics in one such society—the United States—has lately become a rhetoric of stark moral conflict. The factors that turn political arenas into predominantly moral realms, typically marked by exaggerated moral claims and intractable conflict, are the same factors that foster a flight into the moral defense against more deeply embedded forces in the personality (see Chapter Three). This means that, so long as we take the moral struggle at face value, we collude in the effort to distract attention from these hidden forces. In this way, we also collude with the broader movement toward the domination of public and political experience by ever-more intransigent forms of moral (or seemingly moral) conflict.

We have trouble with right and wrong when we associate getting a specific matter "wrong" with "being wrong" in a more fundamental sense. If we fear "being wrong," in this sense, then "wrong" is something that we fear we *are*. One way we can cope is to block awareness of our wrongness by transferring what is wrong about us onto a moral plane, which is the plane on which accepting guilt and pursuing reparation can fix what is wrong and, so, can make us right. Moralizing our sense of fundamental wrongness constitutes a defense against acknowledging the deeper flaw in our personalities, whose presence—or, rather, the acknowledgment of whose presence - would make futile any effort to make ourselves right by acts of will. The prominence of defenses against acknowledging that we are fundamentally wrong—or, in Judith Butler's language, that we are either "un-done" or "missing something" (2004, p. 30)—indicates that, were we able to look into the core of our personalities, we would find there what Michael Balint refers to as a "basic fault."

According to Balint, the basic fault is "an irregularity in the overall structure … something wrong in the mind, a kind of deficiency which must be put right" (1969, p. 21). The basic fault is felt as "emptiness, being lost, deadness, futility, and so on, coupled with an apparently lifeless acceptance of everything that has been offered. In fact, everything is accepted without much resistance but nothing makes sense" (p. 19). While individuals are typically unable to identify "what the fault in them is … [s]ome are capable of expressing it by its opposite, i.e., by fantasies of the perfect partner, or of perfect harmony with their whole environment, perfect untroubled happiness, perfect contentment with themselves and with their world, and so on" (pp. 88–89).

Balint traces the origin of the basic fault "to a considerable discrepancy in the early formative phases of the individual between his bio-psychological needs and the material and psychological care, attention, and affection available during the relevant times" (p. 22). He describes this discrepancy as a defect or deficiency in what he refers to as "primary love." Primary love is a relationship "in which … only one of the partners matters; his wishes and needs are the only ones that count and must be attended to," whereas "the [other] partner," while "felt to be immensely powerful … only matters in so far as he is willing to gratify … needs and desires or decides to frustrate them" (p. 23).

For Balint, "[T]he aim of all human strivings is to establish—or, probably reestablish—an all-embracing harmony with one's environment, to be able to love in peace" (p. 65). Expressed as a wish, this striving takes the following form:

> I must be loved and looked after in every respect by everyone and everything important to me, without anyone demanding any effort or claiming any return for this. It is only my own wishes, interests, and needs that matter; none of the people who are important to me must have any interests, wishes, needs, different from mine, and if they have any at all, they must subordinate theirs to mine, without any resentment or strain; in fact, it must be their pleasure and enjoyment to fit into my wishes. If this happens, I shall be good, pleased, and happy, but that is all. If this does not happen, it will be horrifying both for the world and for me. (pp. 70–71)

In this way, the defect or deficiency in primary love that concerns Balint is similar to what Alice Miller—borrowing insights from Winnicott, Mahler, and Kohut—describes in *The Drama of the Gifted Child*: The asymmetry in power between parent and child is exploited by the (narcissistic) parent, who uses the child to gratify his or her own unmet psychic needs (1997, pp. 33–34). In this situation, the child may receive attention, approval, or other intense and passionate forms of love, but never the kind of love that is appropriate to the true needs of the child. That is, in Miller's words, the child is never loved "in the way he needs to be loved."

> [T]he continuity and constancy that would be so important for the child are missing ... Yet, what is missing above all is the framework within which the child could experience his feelings and his emotions. Instead, he develops something the mother needs, and this certainly saves his life (the mother's or the father's love) at the time, but it nevertheless may prevent him, throughout his life, from being himself. (pp. 34–35)

The fundamental or primary love the child truly "needs" requires attention to the child as a unique and special being, as "the person he really is at any given time"—including moments of rage, sadness, exasperation, and the like—and, perhaps most importantly, "as the center—the central actor—in his own activity" (p. 7).

A defect in primary love means the loss of the feeling that we matter, an inversion of the logic of the world, which changes from a place where we are central to a place where we are merely an appendage of a partner who (alone) matters. If we do not matter in ourselves, but only in as much as we are able to gratify another, then we are of no consequence in ourselves. If we do not matter in ourselves, then neither does anything we do to express our presence in the world. This experience of not mattering even to ourselves becomes an internal quality of our being, which is felt to be defective in a fundamental way: We cannot make anything matter. Hence the feeling of emptiness to which Balint draws our attention.

The notion of a basic fault is a way of thinking about existential anxiety in which emphasis is placed on the experience of a defect in the most significant, vital, or *basic* organ: the self. The idea of a basic fault in the self is linked to the fantasy of a destroyed world because the rupture in the connection Balint refers to as "primary love" has destroyed what constitutes the essential environment, or safe space, needed for the child to develop a healthy sense of self. That a defect in primary love affects not merely the child, or the child–parent relationship, but the whole "environment" (Balint, 1969, pp. 64–72), helps us understand how defects in primary love may be experienced as the destruction not just of an individual but of the entire world.

It needs to be emphasized that the destroyed world is not simply an empty space but a world characterized first by absence, and then by figures and forces that transform it into an actively destructive alternative environment. The destroyed inner world is brought into existence when sufficient damage has been done to the provision of primary love and all it entails. Therefore, the destroyed world is a place in which we can, at best, persist in seeking out primary love and searching for the feelings of security and meaning we associate with it, but where we will never find them.

To understand better the experience of the basic fault, especially as it bears on matters of taking responsibility for harm done, it may be helpful to consider the following example:

> Ethan was an author who had recently published a book of case studies including one featuring a young woman whose work was gaining attention in her field. Ethan included her in the study because of his interest in and regard for her work, both of which he thought came through in the presentation of her case. Shortly after publication, Ethan's publisher received a letter from the young woman alleging that the case study included false statements and threatening to sue Ethan and the publisher for libel. Ethan was shocked and distressed by the accusation, by the threat, and by the significant aggression expressed in them. In his response to his publisher, he made it clear that everything he wrote in his book about the young woman came from public sources, which were duly cited, and that his use of those sources was consistent with the norms

of publication. Nonetheless, Ethan could not dispel the conviction that he had done harm to the young woman, nor could he dispel the guilt attached to that conviction. He had fantasies of sending her a letter saying how sorry he was for having caused her to suffer and making it clear how much he admired her work. These fantasies persisted in spite of the fact that, in reality, Ethan was the victim of aggression and not its source, something about which he was also aware.

Ethan found himself searching for ways that he may have acted on an unconscious intent to damage her, and, therefore, would indeed have been the guilty party. Because it is always possible to find some aggression in situations such as this, and because Ethan's case study was not a simple celebration of the young woman's work but a more in-depth attempt at interpretation, it was not hard to identify at least possible instances in his study that could be experienced as criticism. As he thought about his response to the threatening letter, he became convinced that his response was largely shaped by the effort to protect the young woman, not so much from his damaging study, although that was involved, but from responsibility for her act of aggression directed at him. To protect her, he had taken responsibility for her aggression and for her intent to do harm and, thus, had taken on the guilt that, on any objective basis, belonged to her.

Yet, even as this interpretation of his response gained strength over time, Ethan continued to find himself in a state of some distress over the interaction. Indeed, the interpretation of his response as rooted in the effort to protect the young woman from responsibility for her aggression, by moderating his guilt, seemed to reveal the presence of another source of distress, one considerably more intense and fundamental. What he realized was that, from the beginning, the primary fuel for his distress was not guilt, but the persistent worry that he had, in fact, gotten the facts of the case all wrong, that the young woman was correct in accusing him of having made false statements and of having fabricated the evidence for his interpretation, which was more a flight of fancy than a serious scholarly effort.

Ethan had, in fact, checked his facts more than once, and reworked the case study numerous times in an effort to make sure that it was correct, if not in the interpretation, in the facts on which that interpretation was based. Indeed, Ethan's fears of "getting it wrong" when he was preparing the case drove him to be especially conscientious and may well provide evidence of his own struggle against a persistent fear that there was

> something fundamentally wrong in his work or in himself. His anxiety was so great that he managed at times to convince himself that he was in the wrong in spite of the fact that he knew this was not true. As a result, he avoided rereading his case study and checking once again that the presentation of the facts was accurate because this might lead him to discover that he had, in fact, gotten it wrong. Clearly the young woman's aggression had negatively affected his capacity to distinguish fantasy from reality and had provoked him to doubt the presence in him of a functioning capacity to know what was real and what was not.
>
> As his internal struggle progressed and his awareness of the emotional issues became clearer, his anxiety diminished to the point that he could perform a "reality check" by reviewing his work. In doing so, he could find only one error, which was entirely trivial. He was relieved to discover that he had, indeed, gotten it right. On the basis of Ethan's disclaimer, Ethan's publisher sent a letter to the young woman insisting that, excepting one trivial error, everything in the study was documented and accurate, while also requesting that she list explicitly the false statements she claimed to have found, which she had not done in her threatening letter. No response was received. Evidently, it was the young woman, and not Ethan, who had gotten it wrong.

In reflecting on this account, we are led to conclude that the first phase of Ethan's emotional response to the accusations and threats, the phase in which responsibility was taken to protect the young woman from feeling guilt for her aggression, was essentially a defense against a deeper and considerably more problematic second phase, which involved coping not with guilt, but with the prospect of getting it wrong, and, specifically, with getting her wrong in his assessment. The hope embedded in the first phase was the hope always embedded in guilt, which is that there is something we can do to make things right so that we can relieve the pain of being responsible for doing harm to others.

In this case, if the problem could have been framed as a matter of guilt for harm done, one solution might have been to write a letter apologizing and attempting, through rectifying errors (imagined or real), to repair the damage. In other words, guilt is painful, but it is also fixable. By contrast, coming to know that one has gotten something or someone wrong, in so far as that is understood to provide definitive evidence of being wrong and of the presence of a basic fault in the self, is considerably more painful because it is evidence that the faculty in the mind that would strive to "fix" things by getting them right is, itself, faulty or impaired. If you are wrong in this basic sense, there is nothing you can do about it.

In Ethan's case, the events recounted here called into question his capacity to know what was real and what was not, and with it, his judgment, in the most basic sense of the word. Without the capacity to make meaningful judgments, it is not possible to live in reality; in other words, to exist anywhere but in a wholly internal, made-up space.

Indeed, aggression such as the aggression that made Ethan its target can be driven by the goal of mystifying its target, thus relegating him or her to a psychic space in which the accusations and attributions of badness cannot be realistically assessed or moderated and, therefore, may carry greater weight. If many forms of aggression—including physical aggression but not excluding verbal and emotional aggression—aim to impair the target's capacity to understand and to judge, then we may say that many forms of aggression aim to expose the fault of the self who is the target of aggression, which means, effectively, reveal to the target his or her fundamental wrongness.

Understanding and Absurdity

One of the most important consequences of the presence of a basic fault is the impairment of our ability to understand. The basic fault impedes the development of the capacity to make things fit into a coherent and meaningful narrative or structure. Or, to be precise, the basic fault impedes the development of the capacity to make our own psychic reality cohere with the realities of others and of the world outside. This impediment is the result of the conviction that our emotional experience—indeed, our emotional existence—is faulty, unreliable, and at odds with our environment.

We come to believe that we are incapable of giving expression to our emotions and inner experiences, which means that we cannot make them meaningful or real. So, as Balint notes, where the basic fault is present, "nothing makes sense" because "the basic fault, as long as it is active, determines the forms of object relations available to the individual" (1969, p. 166). Since the basic fault determines how the individual fits his or her psychic reality into the objective, interpersonal world, it powerfully delimits what the individual can understand about him- or herself and about that world.

In his famous essay on the feeling (*sensibilité*) of absurdity, Albert Camus writes:

> A world that can be explained even with bad reasons is a familiar world. But, on the other hand, in a universe suddenly divested of illusions and lights, man feels an

> alien, a stranger. His exile is without remedy since he is deprived of the memory of a lost home or the hope of a promised land. This divorce between man and his life, the actor and his setting, is properly the feeling of absurdity. (1955, p. 6)

While we may disagree with Camus' conclusions about the meaning of absurdity and the most responsible reactions to it, Camus remains an incisive, if unwitting, expositor of the experience of the basic fault and the agonizing disorientation associated with the inability to make sense of one's environment (see also Bowker, 2013, 2014). Camus refers more than once to this experience in the language of "divorce," "exile," and a broken or lost "home."

Indeed, existential and absurd philosophies, such as Camus', may be read as an effort to defend against the basic fault, for the absurd posture discovers in (projects into) the world an inexplicable moral defect responsible for our confusion and pain. In Camus' thought, we find several remarkable similarities to the emotional damage, defective primary love, and inappropriate care and attunement we have discussed throughout this chapter as contributors to the internalization of a basic fault and the development of the fantasy of a destroyed world. For instance, what makes the world absurd, for Camus, is that "the human cry" (*l'appel humain*) confronts "the unreasonable silence of the world" (1955, p. 28). The human cry or the human call—a phrase that is evocative of the predicament of the infant or child who cries out for attention or care—is met with the kind of silence that suggests absence, not only the absence of the parent or caregiver who should hear, but the psychic absence or nonexistence of the one who cries. If we cry and no one responds, our cries do not matter, and, therefore, neither do we. The agonizing result of this predicament, then, is that a defect in primary love, the absence of a secure environment, an absent caregiver, or the loss of a home forces us to confront (too early) our own destruction, our own emotional or psychic nonexistence, our own annihilation.

Although agonizing, the "*mal de l'esprit*" (psychological/intellectual malady) that Camus names "absurdity" must become central to our ways of relating to ourselves and to others (p. 2). That is, according to Camus, we must fully inhabit this defective world of unreasonable silence, without rationalizing its terms. This effort to protect the most basic experience of confusion and disorientation is justified in terms of honesty and fidelity to an emotional experience, about which Camus is famously vague. We are not, writes Camus, to be delivered from our bewilderment, but, rather, must reach the "waterless deserts" of the "distant regions" of the psyche, and then "stay there … to examine closely the odd vegetation" (pp. 9–10). More than once, Camus refers to such regions as "deserts" of the mind (p. 22), even as (intellectually, spiritually) "deadly" climates (p. 29).

What makes the absurd regions so barren, to explore the metaphor, derives, of course, not from any geological property, but from their remoteness from anything familiar, from reason and understanding, from homes or homelands, from belonging and from that which belongs.

For Camus, the self must reject rationalization, acceptance, and all other ways of making sense of the primitive experience of dreadful incomprehension simply because "this is not the way [he (the self)] experienced them. Their truth must be preserved, which consists in not being satisfied" (p. 49). This basic lack of satisfaction (which might also be considered an early and traumatic deprivation) must "be clung to" and "must not be forgotten" because, for Camus, they are so centrally fixed in the psyche that they are all that is felt to be real: "The experiences called to mind here were *born in the desert* that we must not leave behind" (pp. 28–29, *emphasis added*).

Camus' interdiction of understanding, itself, raised in his discussion of G. W. F. Hegel and Mikhail Bakunin, is telling in this respect: "He who has understood reality does not rebel against it, but rejoices in it; in other words, he becomes a conformist" (1956, p. 156). For Camus, we must be aware of acts of destruction, injustices, and atrocities committed in the world. But more important for Camus is that we hold onto the conviction that the destruction we find in the world remains incomprehensible and overwhelming. Life in an absurd world is therefore defined by the activity of seeking out evidence that the destroyed world of our fantasy is real. The irony is, of course, that what is lost in our experience of emotional destruction is the very capacity Camus seems to cherish: the capacity to make contact with our emotions and with what is real in the self. We cling to absurdity, then, as a substitute for self-contact.

Since having "understood reality" means, for Camus, understanding reality in terms other than those of the absurd doctrine, then understanding is tantamount to betraying the experience of emotional destruction to which Camus wishes to be faithful. It also (conveniently) makes one a collaborator with the ubiquitous malevolent forces that populate the destroyed-world fantasy born from the same emotionally destructive experience. It is important, on this line of thought, that the destroyed world remains opaque, that one is never spoken to or attended to. This insistence on absence and silence—such as the famous lament of the "silence of God" (see e.g. Wiesel, 2006)—is crucial to those who inhabit an absurd and destroyed world. To "understand" reality would suggest that one has been spoken to, attended to, communicated with in ways that might help make sense of events and experiences in the world. Those who hear cannot share in the fantasy of incomprehensible, silent torment, so, for Camus, those who understand (or imagine that they understand) come to be identified with the tormentors, themselves.

Read in this light, Camus' defense of absurdity may be read as a defense against the basic fault, or, more aptly, an insistence on the inevitability of it. After all, to the extent that we can be assured that the basically faulty (absurd) environment is shared, essential, and unfathomable, our suspicions of a basic fault in ourselves are allayed: Our basic fault both is and is not our fault. Camus' unwillingness to approach this dilemma in terms of the kind of guilt that could be ameliorated through understanding, taking responsibility, confession, contrition, or acts of reparation is, in one sense, a rejection of the flight into morality that is the subject of this book. On the other hand, as Camus was not a systematic thinker and infused his "absurd logic" with morality to a great degree, Camus effectively moralizes the rejection of morality in the following way: "To make sense of the faulty world is a moral ill, rooted in the 'appetite for clarity' and the 'sin of wanting to know'" (1955, pp. 17, 49). For Camus, to know—or even to want to know—reality is to make "appeals" or concessions to ideas, figures, or others that represent early objects that were not there, and, so, to oppose the effort to make reality match fantasy, which is done by insisting on the reality of their absence.

Søren Kierkegaard's description of the self in "demoniac despair" that strives to make indelible the fault in its environment captures something important about Camus' stance. "Rebelling against all existence," this despairing self "feels that it has obtained evidence against it, against its goodness." Kierkegaard continues:

> The person in despair believes that he himself is the evidence, and that is what he wants to be, and therefore he wants to be himself, himself in his torment, in order to protest against all existence with this torment ... [A]ny consolation ... would be his undoing—as a denunciation of all existence. Figuratively speaking, it is as if an error slipped into an author's writing and the error became conscious of itself as an error—perhaps it actually was not a mistake but in a much higher sense an essential part of the whole production—and now this error wants to mutiny against the author, out of hatred toward him, forbidding him to correct it and in maniacal defiance saying to him: "No, I refuse to be erased; I will stand as a witness against you, a witness that you are a second-rate author." (1980, pp. 73–74)

Here—in an allegory that offers some illuminating resonances with the portrait of Ethan, the accused author, cited above—the self is equated with a disfigured, anthropomorphized "error." In this case, however, the entire psychic and spiritual life of the self is defined by its identification with fault and, therefore, by hatred of itself and of its author or creator. The self in this kind of despair refuses to correct itself or to be corrected—after all, in this metaphor, to erase the error would be to annihilate the entire existence of the self—and, more importantly, lives to exhibit the faultiness of a deficient creator.

In this case, we are reminded again that, despite popular portrayals of destroyed worlds that suggest the opposite, it is not primarily aggression that defines the destroyed world, but absence and all that absence entails. In the excerpt cited just above, the "*absent*-minded" author may or may not have made a slip of the pen, but the error comes to identify so mightily with this absence that it can only find a facsimile of presence and aliveness by repeatedly accusing and derogating the author for his lack of attention and care.

In the chapters that follow, we remark on an absence in the destroyed world represented not only by figures whose presence, paradoxically, stands in for an absence, but in the emptiness, aridity, desolation, and barrenness of landscapes that are not unlike Camus' "deadly climates" and "waterless deserts." While, on one level, violence and harm seem to characterize the (fantasy of) the new world of the American West, what really defines this world is a dangerous emptiness that reflects God's absence. Akin to the writings of Camus and others in the aftermath of the Holocaust, we may learn more about the fantasy of the destroyed world if we are attentive not only to the overt qualities of the narratives presented, but to less obvious laments about the absence of loving, caring, or salvific figures who would rescue us from the deadly climates of our own making.

Note

1. Although we typically employ the pronoun formulations, "he or she," "his or her" or "him- or herself," in this section, for the ease of reading, we have chosen the singular masculine pronouns, "he," "him," and "his." This manner of writing, of course, should not be taken to mean that the (fantasy) experience described here refers only to boys, men, or males, but, rather, to individuals of any sex or gender. A similar but not identical situation will arise in later chapters—and we will address it again there, as well—in our discussions of the "mother," who, while historically associated with females and women, may refer to a caregiver of any sex or gender.

CHAPTER THREE

Guilt and Responsibility

Managing Aggression

According to Freud, "the price we pay for our advance in civilization is a loss of happiness through the heightening of the sense of guilt" (1930a, p. 81). Freud's starting point is the idea that "the prevention of an erotic satisfaction calls up a piece of aggressiveness against the person who has interfered with the satisfaction, and ... this aggressiveness has to be suppressed in turn." The aggressiveness provoked in this way "is transformed into a sense of guilt, by being suppressed and made over to the superego" (p. 85).

Guilt refers to the emotional experience of this redirection of aggression from its original target toward the self. For Freud, this is the psychodynamic process by which pursuit of instinctual satisfaction is repressed so that the bonds of civilization can be established. Creating "a unity out of the individual human beings" requires that "no attention be paid to the happiness of the individual" (p. 87). The aggression that would otherwise threaten the bond holding society together must be redirected inward. To the extent that the individual depends on and requires collective life to attain his or her aims, the work of achieving those aims means giving guilt a prominent place in the individual's inner world.

When Freud refers to the "sense of guilt," he has in mind something different from "the reaction after an act of aggression has already been carried out," which he refers to as "remorse." The sense of guilt differs from remorse in that, whereas remorse refers to the emotional response to a particular act of aggression that actually occurred, the sense of guilt is a "permanent internal unhappiness" (p. 75). This permanent internal unhappiness follows from the way the redirection of aggression, from others toward the self, empowers the superego.

According to Freud, the severity of the superego, in other words the intensity of the sense of guilt, is "simply a continuation of the severity of the external authority, to which it has succeeded and which it has in part replaced" (p. 74). The superego, then, can be considered an internal object relation of a special kind, one bound up with self-repression put in service of relating to others. It is an internalized object relation that develops out of relationships with an "external authority" that assures the child's adaptation of his behavior to the end of securing connections with others and restraining the potentially corrosive effects of aggressive impulses. "External authority" refers, of course, to parents or primary caregivers, terms we will consider interchangeable. So, the process of establishing the superego is one of internalizing parental discipline—discipline informed, of course, by the cultural norms in which the parents (and their parents) have been embedded.

Typically, we conceive of internalizing external authority as a way of replacing external discipline with self-discipline. But the formation of a harsh and repressive internal object relation can also fulfill a need created not by the power and presence of external authority but by its weakness or absence. That is, if the external authority is in some way unreliable, the individual may need to call on an internal authority to compensate for the external authority's deficiency. Furthermore, the less reliable the external authority, the more intense the aggression directed against it for its failure to provide safety, and the more problematic the task of managing aggression. This intensified aggression directed toward the parent may then be redirected toward the self as a way of protecting the parent from it.

Melanie Klein elaborates on the dynamic process by which aggression is redirected toward the self, thereby coming to be experienced as guilt. According to Klein, the "baby's first object of love and hate—his mother—is both desired and hated with all the intensity and strength that is characteristic of the early urges of the baby" (1937, p. 306). The baby loves his mother as the source of satisfaction of bodily needs and as the locus of feelings of safety. "But when the baby is hungry and his desires are not satisfied ... [h]atred and aggressive feelings are aroused and he becomes dominated by the impulses to destroy the very person who is the object of his desires and who in his mind is linked up with everything he experiences—good and bad alike" (pp. 306–307).

Thus, love is "already disturbed at its roots by destructive impulses" (p. 308). Love and hate are now "struggling together in the baby's mind," a struggle that becomes a "source of danger in human relationships." Guilt is the emotional experience of this struggle, the feeling provoked in us when "we detect in ourselves impulses of hate toward the person we love" (p. 309). When the struggle between love and hate becomes active in the psyche, and when the inner world is significantly shaped by the fear of loss of the loved one resulting from fantasized destruction, guilt enters "as an inherent part of love" (p. 311).

An especially important response to the situation in which the baby finds himself is the formation of fantasies. These are pleasant fantasies of the presence and availability of the maternal object; and they are aggressive or destructive fantasies involving attacks on that object for its failure to be available and to provide gratification when needed. Klein emphasizes that, for the baby, these fantasies are *real*, that the fantasized destruction of the maternal object has actually occurred in response to the child's attacks on it. To say that the fantasies are real is simply to point out that the baby, and to a significant degree the young child, lacks a fully developed distinction between fantasy and reality, or possesses a limited capacity to know reality. The more powerful the fantasy of guilt, the more feeling guilty becomes a defining quality of the inner world, which becomes, above all else, the setting for a drama of aggression, harm, and guilt. When this dynamic dominates in relating more generally, guilt becomes a defining factor in larger systems of human relations.

We should note that Klein uses the term "love" in a way distinct from the way it is used when Balint refers to "primary love." The latter term refers to the expectation the child has for a specific kind of object relation marked by exclusivity and the reliability of attention and care. By contrast, when Klein refers to the baby's love for the mother, it is not a question of the baby providing care or attention, only receiving it. The baby's happy response to receiving care is interpreted as love, which here simply means the immediate and uncomplicated emotional response to being connected to the source of drive-satisfaction. But, as Winnicott emphasizes, if this is love, it is a ruthless kind of love, in that the connection to the parent is all about the baby and not at all about the well-being of the parent. Because of this, it is difficult to consider the attitude of the baby toward the mother one of love for the mother. Winnicott suggests as much when he refers to the "developing love of the mother" (1958a, pp. 22–23). This formulation indicates that love is not an original impulse, but something that emerges within the connection to the parent.

Whether love is something that develops or is simply present as a part of the organism's natural endowment depends on the way the aim of love is conceived, specifically whether it is to satisfy an instinctual need, or it comes into existence with the emergence of *concern* for an object (pp. 22–23). When the latter is the case, the development of love parallels the process of the child "becoming a unit ... and being able to perceive the mother as a person." This brings us closer to "primary love," as Balint conceives it. Concern, and therefore the possibility of guilt, are tied to the development of unit status. Without unit status, the essential basis for attaching experience to the presence and action of a person is missing. Without this attachment of experience to the presence and action of a person, there can be no guilt.

Guilt, then, can be considered an aspect of agency. It emerges because of the involvement of the individual in exercising his or her capacity to take responsibility for gratification and for its absence, which includes the taking of responsibility for aggressive (including fantasized) attacks on objects that fail to gratify. Agency stands at the center of what Winnicott refers to as the infantile illusion: the child's fantasy of having the power to create the world (1986, p. 40). The link between guilt and agency or self-determination, then, makes guilt a central feature of social connection in settings where individual self-determination is a defining ideal.

Reparation and Gratitude

The fusion of love and hate fosters a powerful urge to repair damage done, in fantasy, to the loved object. "Side by side with the destructive impulses in the unconscious mind both of the child and of the adult, there exists a profound urge to make sacrifices in order to help and to put right loved people who, in phantasy [unconscious fantasy], have been harmed or destroyed" (Klein, 1937, p. 311). Acting out this fantasy is not limited to the participants in the original relationship, but, rather, becomes part of a paradigmatic orientation toward others for which the early relationship provides the template.

The situation that fosters the experience of guilt and the fantasy of reparation also, according to Klein, fosters another feeling she considers vital to the social bond—gratitude—and an orientation toward others that expresses gratitude—generosity. Klein sees the origin of gratitude in the "relation to the mother's breast," which "becomes the foundation for devotion to people, values, and causes" (1957, p. 187). Considered more broadly, gratitude has its origin in the early provision of a secure and nurturing environment, one where love dominates, even, or especially, in the face of aggression. Such an environment is not assured when aggression is forbidden or punished, but when it is managed in a way that does not threaten the self, when aggression can become a tolerable or safe part of self-experience. In other words, a safe environment is one in which aggression can be integrated into the personality. Alternatively, to redirect aggression toward the self—because its expression is felt to be unsafe—establishes an equation between aggression and self-destruction, making the management of aggression later in life more difficult. Without the capacity to manage aggression while maintaining access to it, there can be no assertion of, and therefore no presence of, the self.

If the parents are unable to manage the child's aggression directed toward them, if they respond with aggression or withdrawal, the child will experience the damaging power of his or her own aggression multiplied, and his or her fantasy of destruction of the loved object realized. The experience of aggression as a powerful force, capable of destroying the connection with the parent and leaving the child helpless and alone, can be managed only by turning aggression back against the self in the way Freud describes. The result of doing so, however, is that aggression against the self comes to dominate the inner world, assuring that it will not be a safe place.

Essential to the development of a capacity for gratitude in adult life is the internalization of the good (gratifying) object, and the consequent predominance in the inner world of the feelings of safety that make the inner world what Winnicott refers to as a "benign environment" (1958b, p. 32). This internalization makes it possible for us to relate to others according to the pattern established in our relationship with a good object, so that "in making sacrifices for somebody we love and in identifying ourselves with the loved person, we play the part of a good parent, and behave towards this person as we felt at times the parents did to us—or as we wanted them to do" (Klein, 1937, pp. 311–312). The internalization of a benign environment fosters the development not of harshly punitive internal objects, but of empathic objects. The result is the internalization of an object relation that fosters gratitude, rather than guilt, as the dominant reality of relating.

Responsibility and the Moral Defense

As we have emphasized, there can be no guilt without a sense of responsibility and, therefore, without agency. For responsibility and guilt to arise, the connection with the maternal object must become something different from what it was originally: an immersion in an indivisible unit. It must encompass the presence of subjectivity or agency, which can only happen when the indivisible unit has given way to a relationship. Agency expresses the presence of the individual as a separate center of emotional experience and leads to the development of a sense of personal responsibility. At the risk of stating the obvious, personal responsibility means, literally, that a person is responsible. In primitive object relations, there are two persons: the child and the parent. Thus, one of the two must be the cause of the gratification or frustration the child experiences.

This attribution of personal responsibility underlies the whole dynamic of causation embedded in the relationship between the child and the parent, subsequently internalized as an object relation an important aspect of which is the sense of guilt. Because love is a relationship between two persons, however primitive the separation of persons may be, it can be said that guilt is an expression of love. If love is an attachment to a person, and, more precisely, to his or her vital presence of being, then love also entails attachment to the aggression that is a requisite part of separate being. That is, although it is sometimes expressed in that way, love cannot be understood merely as the urge to overcome separation and aggression, for without separation and aggression, love is not possible.

At the same time, guilt is not only an expression of agency and, therefore, of the presence of the self; it is also an attack on the seat of agency that is the self. Guilt expresses both the presence of the self—the center of initiative and emotional experience—and the impulse to repress the self, because the emotional experience of having a self comes to be identified with an attack on the connection with the good object. This expression of self in its negation fits with an emotional bond that attaches the individual to a social order in a way that involves a significant measure of repression driven by a fundamental suspicion of the self.

Its link to self-repression does not, however, imply that self-determination is inherently at odds with a social order in which guilt plays a part, as Freud suggests that it is. Much depends on the kind of guilt that shapes the social bond. Specifically, it matters whether we are dealing with the kind of guilt that fosters a fundamental distrust of all expressions of the self, or the kind of guilt that expresses the value placed on the presence of the self in the world by signaling that harm to the self-in-other has been done and repair is needed. This distinction is also the distinction between guilt assumed for harm done by the individual and guilt taken on for harm done by others, or by no one at all.

Underlying the expansion of guilt beyond harm done is the internal struggle over the bad or guilty self. The power of the fear that the self is always and irrevocably bad indicates the presence of a guilty self, which is not the same as the capacity for guilt. When "the subject ... cannot admit of any wrongdoing or badness without being revealed as a poisonously all-bad object" (Carveth, 2001), guilt takes on the special form with which we are concerned here. Fear that we will be identified with an all-bad object is fear that we will become, in ourselves, irredeemably bad and therefore unworthy of love. Identification with an all-bad internal object, then, fosters a way of managing guilt that has important consequences for the shape that social institutions and systems of relating adopt.

The struggle with this identification is the central element in Ronald Fairbairn's (1952) notion of the "moral defence." In speaking of the moral defense, Fairbairn notes that, while "the delinquent child is reluctant to admit that his parents are bad objects, he by no means displays equal reluctance to admit that he himself is bad. It becomes obvious, therefore, that the child would rather be bad himself than have bad objects; and accordingly, we have some justification for surmising that one of his motives in becoming bad is to make his objects 'good.'" By doing so, the child seeks to "purge" his objects of their badness, "and in proportion as he succeeds in doing so, he is rewarded by that sense of security which an environment of good objects invariably confers." To say that the child takes on this "burden of badness" is "the same thing as to say that he internalizes bad objects" (p. 65). Fairbairn goes on to point out that this taking on the burden of badness, or internalizing bad objects, if it makes the world outside a safe place, does so by making the inner world an unsafe place.

Fairbairn then develops an important distinction between those objects that are unconditionally bad and those that are conditionally bad.

The unconditionally bad objects are "simply persecutors," while the conditionally bad objects are "bad from a moral standpoint." Conditionally bad objects are bad from the standpoint of an internalized good object. So far as the child is identified with his unconditionally bad objects, he becomes unconditionally bad. To offset this situation, the child takes "what is really a very obvious step. He internalizes his good objects, which thereby take on a super-ego role" (p. 66). As a result, the internal situation becomes one marked by conditional badness and conditional goodness. So far as the child has internalized a good object to stand against the bad, he has internalized the seat of judgment of good and bad, which means that he can be good, or not, depending on the extent to which he follows this internal judgment.

From this, Fairbairn concludes that "it is obviously preferable to be conditionally good than conditionally bad; but, in default of conditional goodness, it is preferable to be conditionally bad than unconditionally bad." Fairbairn formulates this situation in a religious language, noting how "it is better to be a sinner in a world ruled by God than to live in a world ruled by the devil." This is due to the fact that in the "world ruled by the devil, the individual may escape the badness of being a sinner; but … he can have no sense of security and no hope for redemption. The only prospect is one of death and destruction" (p. 67). Fairbairn goes on to note that the child does not have the option of simply rejecting his bad objects because he "cannot do without them." Indeed, "even if they neglect him, he cannot reject them; for, if they neglect him, his need for them is increased" (p. 67).

As a result of this complex shaping of the inner world, it now becomes necessary to do something about the badness there. As we will see further on, the cost of adopting the moral defense—which Fairbairn also refers to as "the defence of guilt"—includes an intensification of aggression toward the self, which can be relieved if the internal bad objects can be moved outside, through projection, into suitable containers there. This is, however, a never-ending project precisely because of the necessity that prompted the original internalization of the bad object.

In the language of the self, this situation can be described in the following way. Only in so far as the self remains alive in the personality can there be any hope for redemption, for only in so far as the self remains alive is there anything to redeem. And only in so far as the self remains alive in the personality is there any possibility of taking responsibility for the badness in the world, since taking responsibility means finding the seat of initiative and action *inside*; which is to say, experiencing the self as a causal factor in doing and relating. Thus, to be unconditionally bad is to have a bad self, which is a contradiction in terms, since the bad self is, in essence, a self devoted to self-destruction, a dead self whose only purpose is to bring death and destruction to itself and to the self as it is imagined to exist outside, in others. For those who are intrinsically or unconditionally bad, there can be no guilt, and therefore no possibility for the repair of, or return of, the self.

The characters in the fantasy representing the moral defense appear in forms that are morphologically similar to the archaic objects and object relations that set the pattern for them, but differ from them in concrete form. The internalized early relationship is projected onto present-day figures having qualities that enable them to stand in for the original objects. Specifically, the original maternal object, whose innocence is meant to be protected by the moral defense, now appears in the form of individuals and groups who, along an important dimension, exhibit the same qualities that define that object. Notably, it may be represented by women generally (all women), or it may be represented by those who are the victims of aggression. In principle, anyone who must be held innocent of responsibility for aggression can be a surrogate or stand-in for the object whose goodness was originally secured by the moral defense.

This way of experiencing all relationships that are morphologically similar to the original object relation extends the sphere of application of the moral defense, which becomes a principle that governs relating in many, possibly all, conditions, such that all objects encountered in reality are experienced as characters in the fantasy driving the moral defense. When this happens, the guilt taken on to protect the innocence of the good object expands exponentially as the individual driven by the moral defense takes responsibility for all violent acts directed at innocent victims, and as he or she is driven by the conviction that the victims of violent acts, when similar to the characters in fantasy, must be innocent. And they must be innocent for the same reason that the good object must be innocent, because, if they are not, then the world is not ruled by God, and there is no hope that the world will be a place in which we can live.

The moral defense, then, is the defense against the prospect of living in a godless world, a world where there is no subject capable of protecting the good and securing its presence. The emotional response to this prospect is not guilt, but rage and despair. Taking responsibility, or accepting guilt, is a strategy put in place to manage feelings of rage and despair. If one becomes guilty, the consequence, or punishment, is that the capacity for action can only be exercised against the self (within) and in defense of the innocent self that has been projected outside. The feeling attached to this situation is a bottomless sense of loss.

Reparative Omnipotence

People take responsibility for things they did not do because they did do them in fantasy and there is, for them, no clearly established distinction between fantasy and reality, therefore no well-defined sphere of reality. Taking responsibility, under these circumstances, can be said to represent the refusal to accept and fully acknowledge reality. This is well expressed in the insistence that there is always something we can do to fix what is wrong in the world and in ourselves, which is another way of saying that there exists nothing beyond our power or outside our control. And we say this because, if it is not true, then we cannot repair our inner world through good work done in the world outside. Guilt is, therefore, at the center of this struggle because guilt is the emotional experience that (1) insists on responsibility for damage done to the good, and (2) drives reparation. In this sense, taking responsibility and feeling guilt indicate the presence of hope.

Just as guilt may or may not be tied to real acts, so also may reparation be tied not to finite and limited forms of guilt, but to guilt for fantasized damage done to fantasy objects. In the latter case, the harm for which we suffer guilt has become a defining feature of our personalities. The more definitive the harm in this sense, the more definitive the guilt, and the more all-encompassing the work needed to repair the damage done. At the limit, the (fantasized) harm can be so great that no reparation is possible.

A fantasy of the definitive destruction of the good object can be managed with an equally definitive destruction of the self. While this act may not restore the object, as the fantasy allows for no repair or return, it will destroy the self, which is the cause of the harm and the target of guilty feelings. This is one possibility. Another is to deny that destruction is irreversible, and to meet (what is imagined to be) the overwhelming magnitude of the act of destruction with a fantasy of omnipotence: "[T]o the feeling of sadistic omnipotence corresponds the feeling of reparative omnipotence" (Klein, 1945, p. 410). The greater the fantasized damage, the greater the fantasized power needed to repair it. In fantasy, of course, there are no limits that constrain either the damage that can be done or the possibility of repair. The power of evil to destroy the world is met with an equal power of good to destroy evil, even to bring the dead back to life. The greater the need to repair damage assumed to be irreparable, the more powerful the impulse to seek refuge in fantasy, where no damage is beyond repair.

We have, then, two additional modalities of guilt and reparation. In one, the damage done and the guilt for doing it are definitive. The self is extinguished and no repair is possible. In the other, the only recourse is to substitute fantasy for reality by meeting the fantasized omnipotence of destructive powers with a fantasy of reparative omnipotence. The outcome of the second modality is a life devoted to the frantic, all-consuming activity of repair, repair that can never succeed in meeting its hidden goal, which is to atone for the fantasized act of destruction that led to the irreversible loss of the good object. Real objects in the external world are treated as if they were the original object destroyed in fantasy. But, because they are stand-ins for the fantasy object, their repair cannot solve the problem for which it was intended. So, reparation in the real world must be endlessly repeated. Reparation turns into penance for original sin.

There is one difference between the two modalities of guilt and repair that has special importance. For the second, unlike the first, the presence of the self matters, even if all it matters for is the repair of the self-in-others. After all, our manic involvement with reparation can also be considered an involvement, via projection, with the repair of our selves. This is not only the repair of our selves through the cleansing power of reparation, but the fantasized repair of the self that has been relocated through projection onto others. In other words, the care we bestow on others is the wished-for care for ourselves we cannot have because we have made ourselves the source of the damage to the object that took those who would care for us out of our world. Here, penance appears very much like generosity, although it is not; and compassion reveals itself as care for the self, rather than the expression of gratitude felt for the care received from a good parent.

The complex relationship between reparation and different forms of guilt reappears as a complexity in the notion of civic engagement and in the insistence on the moral imperative to participate in civic life where we may be told: "Everyone can do something." "There is always something we can do." Or, "Something must be done." To the extent that the imperative to participate expresses the conviction, or at least the hope, that participation evinces or even creates moral character, participation may be motivated by the kind of guilt that fosters manic forms of reparation. Indeed, guilt and manic reparation are not just motives for participation, but also factors in the psyche struggling to find expression by way of participation. This raises the question: When we participate, are we seeking participation by, and involvement of, the self? Or, are we seeking participation by, and involvement of, factors in the personality responsible for repression of the self? What internal object relations, as expressed in unconscious fantasy, are we seeking to activate by calling for participation? In the following chapters, we explore these and other closely related questions.

CHAPTER FOUR

Guilty Selves and Social Systems

Self-Determination, Group Life, and Hate

Guilt becomes important in defining social connection and social order when two conditions are met: (1) Individual self-determination, and the implied presence of a separate self, plays a significant role in social connection, so that personal responsibility is an active factor in relating, and (2) distrust of the self is among the social order's preeminent features. This means, in particular, that guilt plays an important role when the submersion of the self into the group cannot be taken for granted because the presence of the self is too powerful, and the group is no longer considered the only or inevitable context for social connection. It is only in societies where being connected means something other than being a part of a group that guilt plays the role considered here. When the presence of the self is too powerful, and when being oneself is equated with being identified with a bad object, the group may become a vehicle for self-repression. Through group connection, it is hoped that connection with the good can be reestablished and guilt can be dismissed. The dynamic described here is played out as a struggle between losing the self into the group and living a life expressive of self-determination.

The power of self-determination means that participation in group life is a choice that must be made, and for which the individual must take responsibility. Participation, therefore, rests on the availability of the option to exist outside the group. The possibility of existing outside the group promotes the use of guilt to block the exercise of that opportunity, that is, to have a life defined not by group identity but by individual expression and achievement. The need to mobilize guilt in response to the conviction of the intrinsic badness of the self is therefore proportional to the power of individual autonomy in social systems that are based both on self-determination and on distrust and repression of the self.

In social systems of this kind, there is a tendency to confuse containment of emotion with repression, with the consequence that the boundary between self and other, established through the exercise of the capacity to hold our emotional states inside, is poorly established. When this capacity is poorly established, so is the assignment of responsibility for our actions and their consequences. Guilt is, then, set loose from its moorings in a clear understanding of the reality of cause and effect, and the foundation is established for the use of guilt to repress the self rather than to indicate that the self is alive and active in doing and relating.

In this struggle over self-determination, envy of those who would live outside the group can play an important role. The possibility of being outside the group means that *existing* in Winnicott's sense of the term is possible (1986, pp. 39–41). Envy of those who claim this possibility and seek to exist outside the group expresses the unconscious knowledge of those who remain in the group that they *do not exist*. Guilt, then, may be understood as the way the group punishes its members for imagining themselves to exist in their own right. To allow members to have a life outside the group diminishes the group in the most essential way and must be resisted with all the power the group has available, especially the power of guilt. Thus the imposition of guilt on those outside the group is the way it seeks to punish them for claiming the right to exist.

But, living outside the group is only possible when the individual has internalized the relationship with the good object so that a connection with an external good object—the group—is no longer essential for a sense of security in being. The less effective the internalization of the good object and creation of a benign inner world, the more powerful the destructive impulse toward the self. Similarly, the less effective the internalization of the good object, the more powerful and more tenuous the hold guilt has over relating.

What makes the hold of guilt tenuous is the relative weakness of the connection to, or experience of, the good object. Without a secure attachment to, and internalization of, the good object, harm done to that object will not provoke feelings of concern or impulses to protect. Because guilt expresses both love and hate, the weaker the love for the object, the less guilt will be felt for destructive impulses directed at it. At the limit, when hate eclipses love, guilt is no longer a factor at all. No one feels guilt for harm they have done to someone for whom they feel nothing but hate. For this reason, it is possible for hate to act as a defense against guilt, especially when hate can be justified by the judgment that hate's object is beyond redemption, that it is the locus of all that is bad in the world, which is to say that hate's object is the (unconditionally) bad self.

Because, as we have seen, there is no love that can be free of guilt, love itself may be experienced as the cause of guilt, which makes love something against which we must defend ourselves, most notably by calling on hate as a replacement for it. The use of hate as a defense against love creates a separation between persons that is sometimes confused with the separation associated with the self-determination that makes life outside the group possible. The result of this confusion is the identification of hate for others with the pursuit of a robust interest in and concern for the self. This confusion is also embedded in the use of those who live outside the group as containers for the bad object.

The Guilty Self

Having or being a guilty self is not the same as the experience of guilt: a temporary activation of the capacity for taking responsibility for harm done. It is not simply the capacity for guilt that is at stake, but the potential for guilt to take over the personality and become its central defining feature. When this happens, we have a self that is defined by guilt rather than by the capacity to take responsibility for harm done. The guilty self is, then, a self that identifies with its guilt and only exists, or only experiences its existence, when taking on guilt and feeling guilty.

Central to the guilty self is the impulse to expand, potentially without limit, responsibility for the bad things that happen in the world around it. This means that the guilty self has a weak connection to the reality of responsibility and to reality-based connections between cause and effect. Instead, the guilty self assumes that harm done (anywhere) is sufficient evidence of responsibility. Wherever it finds harm done, it finds an opportunity to take responsibility. Because of this seeking-after-responsibility, the individual possessed of a guilty self can always be made to feel responsible for what is bad in the world and may be driven to share that feeling with or impose that feeling on others. Yet, as it turns out, the guilty self is not consumed by real guilt, but by a facsimile of guilt, put in place to protect the personality from a greater threat.

As an example, consider the following exchange between James Baldwin and Margaret Mead (1971). The topic is the Sixteenth Street Baptist Church bombing in 1963, a racially motivated attack in Birmingham, Alabama that killed four girls. In this exchange, Mead asks Baldwin: "Did you bomb those little girls in Birmingham?" Baldwin's response is: "I'm responsible for it. I didn't stop it." The conversation proceeds:

> Mead: Why are you responsible? Didn't you try to stop it? Hadn't you been working?
>
> Baldwin: It doesn't make any difference what one's tried.
>
> Mead: Of course it makes a difference what one's tried.
>
> Baldwin: No, not really.
>
> Mead: This is the fundamental difference. You are talking like a member of the Russian Orthodox Church: "We are all guilty. Because some man suffers, we are all murderers."
>
> Baldwin: No, no, no. We are all responsible.
>
> Mead: Look, you are not responsible.
>
> Baldwin: That blood is also on my hands.
>
> Mead: Why?
>
> Baldwin: Because I didn't stop it.
>
> Mead: Is the blood of somebody who is dying in Burma today on your hands?
>
> Baldwin: Yes, yes.
>
> Mead: Because you didn't stop that? That's what I mean by the Russian Orthodox position, that all of us are guilty of all that has been done or thought.
>
> Baldwin: Yes.
>
> Mead: And I will not accept it. I will not ... I will not accept responsibility for what other people do because I happen to belong to that nation or that race or that religion. I do not believe in guilt by association.

In this dialogue, we see two contradictory standpoints. In one, individuals feel responsible not just for themselves but for the entire world. In the other, individuals accept that there are limits to their responsibility, that there are others with different and independent subjectivities whom they do not control and for whose actions they cannot be held responsible. For the former, unlimited responsibility involves one in a paradox where the individual is responsible for everything, and must do or must have done everything, but is simultaneously incapable of doing anything that is properly his or her own. For the latter, this setting of limits on control and responsibility means that there are things they cannot do, but also that there are things they *can* do.

Baldwin faces the world from the first standpoint. He insists that, although he did not cause suffering around the globe, and in that sense is not guilty, he is responsible for it. He is responsible because he did not prevent it; he did not keep the innocent safe. To make the distinction and the focus of the discussion clear, Mead offers the following definition of responsibility with which Baldwin concurs: Responsibility "is saying I am going to make an effort to have things changed." We should note that this differs significantly from the usual definition of responsibility, which does not refer to what you say you are going to try to do, but to what you are capable of doing. Normally, responsibility indicates that you are "liable to be called to account as the primary cause, motive, or agent" (*Merriam-Webster's Collegiate Dictionary*, 2006). What is important about the element of being a cause or agent in the definition of responsibility is that it highlights the link between responsibility and capability. If you caused harm to another, then evidently you were capable of doing so, as the exercise of that capability is a necessary condition for causation to apply. Similarly, if you fail to prevent harm that you could have prevented, then you can be considered responsible for the harm done. But, it is clear from the way Baldwin speaks about responsibility that this condition does not apply for him, at least not in any simple or straightforward way.

There is, however, a way to understand Baldwin's position that makes it consistent with the usual meaning of responsibility. This is not through a redefinition of responsibility but through considering more closely what agency means to him. Baldwin can speak about his personal responsibility in the way he does because the "self" to which he refers when he takes responsibility is not the personal identity attached to his unique presence of being, but a self disconnected from his personal agency, his unique life trajectory, indeed even his personal presence. His way of thinking about responsibility expresses his conviction not only that a self separated from personal presence exists, but that it is he. In a way, just as his words in this conversation suggest a conviction about the expanded significance of his presence in the world, and therefore of his expanded responsibility, they are also a kind of appeal to his nonexistence as a personal or individual subject.

To the extent that he is making an appeal to his nonexistence, his notion of responsibility embodies his insistence that attention must not be paid to the "I" that refers uniquely to him. But, it also indicates an expansion of his agency without limit in time, place, and circumstance: He is nowhere in particular; and he is everywhere. Baldwin's message can be summed up in the following way: "To refuse to take responsibility is to insist on separate or personal existence. To insist on separate or personal existence is what makes you responsible for the suffering in the world because it separates you from, and inures you to, the suffering of others, making you either indifferent to it or the beneficiary of it, which is, in itself, a kind of harm, or, even, the very meaning of harm."

We can see this message clearly expressed in the exchange with Mead. Baldwin insists, and Mead concurs, that "everybody's suffering is mine," which also means that their personal suffering would hold no special significance for themselves.

> Mead: Look, there have been millions of crimes committed against humanity. Millions! Now, why is one crime more important than another?
>
> Baldwin: No, my point precisely is that one crime is not more important than another and that all crimes must be atoned for.

Mead goes so far as to say that she does "not distinguish for one moment whether my child is in danger or a child in Central Asia."

There is a sense in which, by taking responsibility for all the suffering in the world, what Baldwin expresses is not the conviction that he caused the event that destroyed the world (the goodness in it), but that he *is* that event. He is the child who awakens in a destroyed world and comes to the conclusion that the world has been lost because he is in it. He then concludes that the only hope he has is to take responsibility for destruction and, moreover, that taking responsibility will, in itself, reverse the loss of the world. Thus, the exchange between Mead and Baldwin is really an exchange about taking responsibility for the destroyed world.

> Baldwin: The world is scarcely habitable for the conscious young ... There is a tremendous national, global, moral waste.
>
> Mead: I know.
>
> Baldwin: And the question is, how can it be arrested? That's the enormous question. Look, you and I both are whatever we have become, and whatever happens to us now doesn't really matter. We're done. It's a matter of the curtain coming down eventually. But what should we do about the children? We are responsible; so far as we are responsible at all, our responsibility lies there, toward them. We have to assume that we are responsible for the future of this world.
>
> Mead: That's right.
>
> Baldwin: What shall we do? How shall we begin it? How can it be accomplished? How can one invest others with some hope?

Underlying this whole exchange is the question: "What can we do?" And, the answer to the question seems to be: "What we can do is take responsibility."

If we can consider this displacement in relation to the moral defense discussed above, it might suggest that taking on limitless responsibility is a strategy for refusing to acknowledge the damage done to you by the good object and the way this was managed by taking responsibility for it. You cannot atone for damage done to you by your parent, damage for which you have taken responsibility precisely because you did not do it. But, you can endlessly repeat the act of taking responsibility in an effort to protect the parent's innocence. And, as it turns out, taking responsibility, in this case, is, in itself, the act that alleviates harm. We relieve others of guilt by taking on their guilt, which is one way of understanding social justice: as the process of relieving those accused of a crime from their responsibility for it, of turning guilt into innocence.

Where the moral defense is involved, the child takes responsibility for the damage done to the child by the adult, thus relieving the parent of guilt at the expense of the child's innocence. The act of taking responsibility is meant, in itself, to solve the problem posed by parental failure. This act of displacement must be repeated over and over again because only by repetition can innocence be maintained against the pressure of the reality that the parent is not innocent. Repetition is meant to protect us from the internal pressure created by the disavowed memory of the badness of the good object and the dreaded consequences of acknowledging that badness. As Fairbairn reminds us, knowing we live in a godless world is worse than taking responsibility for the badness in that world.

Taking on guilt can be a defense against intolerable emotional states associated with the loss of a world and the intense destructive impulses provoked by that loss. Because intense destructive impulses can be provoked by the loss of a safe space or a safe world, the latter may come to be causally linked to the former, such that the impulse to destroy the world can be merged with the absence of safe space. As we have seen, there is an important distinction to be drawn between the loss of a world and its destruction.

In primitive emotional life, "the world" is our experience of being in the presence (both physical and emotional) of our primary caregivers. This means that the loss of the world is the loss (or absence) of emotional and physical connection. Similarly, the "destruction of the world" is an act (real or imagined) that took caring connections and caregivers away from us. It is important to remember that this loss or destruction also entails the loss or destruction of connection with our selves.

Subjective Causation and Harmful Intent

So far as the effort to make sense of the loss and/or destruction of connection to ourselves and to those on whom we depend involves recourse to a primitive notion of causation, it is inevitable that we interpret the loss of the world on the basis of harmful intent: "Someone made it happen." And, in so far as "making it happen" means acting on destructive impulse, the questions that must be resolved are: "Where does the destructive impulse lie?" and, "Who bears responsibility for it?" By assigning responsibility, we identify a path to reversing the damage and thereby to defending ourselves against the inevitability/irreversibility of the destruction of the world. That is, insisting on responsibility for all events is, in many ways, more significant than assigning responsibility for any particular event to any particular party. The insistence on responsibility for all events—whether it is ultimately the self who ends up bearing the guilt, or another party, or all people taken together, or even a fluid combination of these—is, in essence, the core conviction of the guilty self.

Thus, we may say that two primary forces drive the logic of subjective causation (Levine, 2017), which entails the belief that all harm is done by a doer with harmful intent: (1) hope for repair or renewal, and (2) managing guilt. If they result in the consolidation of a guilty self, hope for repair and painful guilt feelings generated in the wake of the loss of our world may lead us away from, not closer to, the redemption we seek.

The power of the idea that all harm done is harm caused by someone derives both from the rule of subjective causation in primitive emotional life and from the nature of early damage to the self. As both Kohut and Winnicott emphasize, it is in the setting of intersubjective experience that the connection to the self is either nurtured or broken. In intersubjective experience, the loss of connection to the self, which is what we mean by damage to the self, is our internal response to the danger our connection to the self poses. If our relationships with our caregivers are dangerous, or if we have no sustaining relationship with them, then the inner world shaped by the internalization of those relationships will become a dangerous place to be as well.

In a very real sense, the damage to the self caused by the internalization of a damaging relationship or relationships is damage caused by another self or subject. It is not surprising, then, that the damage done to the self in its effort to exist in the world is construed as someone's responsibility, and therefore someone's fault, that someone is the guilty party. Yet, from early on, this guilty party has two faces and is subject to two different—and each in its own way valid—interpretations: The guilty party is ourselves and it is someone else. Guilty are those whose ways of relating to us make being and relating unsafe. And, guilty are we in that once the dangerous relationship has been internalized, it continues to exist in the absence of others.

The internalization of damaging object relations has a further consequence: It makes responsibility for harm done to the self in the inner world an enduring reality of that world as expressed in the obsessive repetition of fantasies featuring relationships in which we are found guilty or find ourselves guilty. This obsessive repetition of fantasy is what we mean when we speak of the guilty self. The more intense the emotion attached to the fantasy and the more space it occupies in the inner world, the more we become a guilty self. And, the more we turn in the direction of being a guilty self, the more powerful the impulse to rid ourselves of the pain felt for knowing that is what we are.

The guilty self, once it becomes the dominant shape of the self, has damaging consequences for individuals and for the groups and societies they inhabit. When responsibility for damage falls on ourselves, we may seek to find the subject or subjects who did the damage to us outside, and this need to find guilty parties outside enhances our dependence on the logic of subjective causation: that someone is always responsible for what has happened to us in the past, for what happens to us in the present, and for what will happen to us in the future. This logic predominates in groups that activate or rely heavily on the evocation of the guilty selves of members.

Guilty Selves and the Quest for Justice

If the guilty self is not synonymous with the capacity for guilt, and if the guilty self is a deformation of the self, it will be worth considering why the self follows the path that leads in the end to its own impairment. One answer is that the idea of a guilty self can apply not only to individual psychology but also, more broadly, to social systems when they are organized to assure that the inner worlds of their members will be configured around a guilty self. This is evidenced by shared fantasies in which self-expression is equated with self-destruction.

A social system organized around the creation and perpetuation of guilty selves will inevitably exhibit an excess of aggression, disruptive tendencies affecting families and society as a whole, powerful impulses driving individuals to seek refuge in groups having the potential to regress into "gangs," and sharp divisions mapping guilt and innocence onto target groups chosen to bear responsibility. The perpetuation of this system is assured by the disruptive potential of the guilty self in the inner world, which translates into the "broken home" syndrome discussed in Chapter Nine, threatening to make society a stage for the enactment of dramas of destruction.

The guilty self needs a world shaped to fit its constituting fantasy, a world divided into the innocent and the guilty, victims who suffer harm and those who cause them harm. It is in such a world that the guilty self finds its home, in so far as the guilty self can be said to have a home. The guilty self is not simply a static presence, but a dramatic enactment. And, therefore, the place in which the guilty self feels at home is not a location in the world but an enactment, or system of enactments, of a defining drama. All institutions are imbued with the logic that governs the drama of guilt and innocence, which is the logic of subjective causation: that there is always someone responsible for damage to the self, and, therefore, that damage can only be repaired if those who have caused it are made to take responsibility for the harm they have done; in other words, someone must always bear the burden of guilt.

Guilt and innocence, as categories of emotional life, bear a complex relation to those categories as they appear in the world outside, especially the world outside of intimate relationships. Yet, the links between guilt and justice must be understood if we are to understand the meaning and significance of the way those categories appear in the outside world. The distinction just drawn is exemplified in the movement from guilt understood as an emotional experience to guilt understood as a legal category. Thus, you may be found guilty in a court of law for doing harm to others, but this does not mean that you experience the feeling of guilt and, in that sense, have the emotional knowledge of your culpability. The legal definition of guilt assigns responsibility or blame, but it cannot impose any feeling of guilt on those found guilty; it cannot make the legally guilty person feel bad, however powerful may be the wish that it could.

This does not, however, exclude the possibility that systems of justice will be built on the belief that their power to adjudicate guilt and innocence also creates in them the power to control the emotional experience of guilt. On the contrary, systems of justice are typically meant to shift the adjudication of guilt, as an internal matter, onto an external authority, and to substitute punishment as a matter of law for the punishment we impose on ourselves as a result of the formation of an internal authority. Psychologically, the purpose of the institutions of justice is typically to instantiate the fantasy that the internal judge either does not exist, or can be replaced by, a power in the external world. This is the fantasy of justice, which is part of a larger fantasy that the emotional experience of the presence in the mind of harsh internal object relations can be dismissed by enacting internal dramas in the world outside, so long as suitable surrogates can be found there. The justice system is meant to identify those surrogates for us.

So far as justice is conceived in the language of innocence, guilt, crime, and punishment, it mirrors the phenomenon of guilt experienced in the inner world, and, because of this, can be said to extend that phenomenon to a world of strangers. Doing so expresses the more general need to have available an external constraint on conduct in settings where guilt is not generated by harm done to others, either because the sense of guilt is impaired or because the emotional connection required to activate the sense of guilt does not exist.

The line of argument suggested by Freud involves thinking about justice systems as substitutes for the superego for those people whose conduct suggests the absence of adequate internal constraints on destructive impulses or who find themselves in settings where their capacity for guilt is not activated. When a system of justice operates in this way, it will parallel the superego in the sense that the nature of punishment will depend on the quality of the punitive internal objects characteristic of the society or culture in which it is embedded. Thus, the more punitive the internal fantasies of crime and punishment present in those who design and administer it, the harsher the system of justice; and, the more benign the inner worlds of those who design and administer the system of justice, the greater the emphasis on reparation, including the repair of the inner worlds of those who commit crimes.

The fantasy sometimes referred to as "frontier justice" (alluded to in Chapter One and taken up again, in a related context, in Chapter Eight) entails the imposition of the harshest punishment on criminals guilty of the most heinous crimes. Frontier justice is the most primitive form of justice, a form applied where the institutions of justice are poorly developed, or not developed at all. Here, justice appears primarily in the form of the individual "lawman," as legal and penal institutions recede into the background. The main punishment takes the form of shooting or hanging those judged by the lawman to be guilty.

In this world, criminals feel no remorse, and therefore know no internal constraint on the expression of their destructive impulses. Because of this, they mirror the absence of constraint on the imposition of justice by lawmen. In the fantasy, the two aspects of guilt we have discussed are separated from each other and projected outside: the factor in the personality that feels nothing for those it harms, and the factor that seeks to restrain the urge to do harm through aggression turned inward. These two factors of the personality are assigned to different persons (outlaws and lawmen); in other words, as is typical in fantasy, factors of the personality are personified. This dynamic process, through which an internal struggle between the remorseless factor in the personality (hate) and the remorseful factor (love) is created in the world outside as a battle between persons, shapes and perpetuates social institutions and relations suited to the mirroring demanded by projection of a harsh and sharply divided inner world.

Central here is the matter of whether the badness with which the justice system is meant to deal is conditional or unconditional, or put another way, whether the justice system conceives of badness as conditional or unconditional. The more badness is conceived to be unconditional, the less relevant will be notions involving reform and repair, and the more emphasis will be placed on harsh and dehumanizing forms of punishment, especially death. In this case, the justice system can be understood as the external manifestation of a psychic formation of a particular kind, a kind of group psyche organized around a fantasy of the remorseless destruction of the self.

The fantasy centered on managing a remorseless self through the imposition of a harsh form of justice suggests how narratives of guilt and innocence can act as defenses against a destroyed world, and therefore how the idea of justice can engage such narratives. Taking responsibility for loss means finding the destructive force in the self, which makes the self responsible for the loss of a world in which it is possible to exist. But, if that destructive force is imagined to be so powerful that it cannot be allowed to survive, then the inner world can only become a dead place, given over to destruction rather than to the nurturance of life.

On the emotional level, the justice system and the ideal of a just society are understood to exist for the purpose of defending, via the imposition of a narrative of innocence, guilt, and punishment, the good object and the safe space around it from chaos and destruction. The imposition of this narrative uses guilt as a defense against the experience of the emotional consequences of the destruction of the world, while providing a surrogate for the good object that offers security in its absence. This surrogate embodies an intensity of fear and aggression, and therefore, in its way, represents the threat to security as much as it represents our defense against the chaos of a destroyed world.

The drama to which we have just referred bears a special connection to loss of the good object. The formation of a harsh superego appears here as a response to absence rather than presence. In other words, it is not primarily the experience of a harsh external authority that matters, but the absence of a good object. Indeed, the presence of the parent in the form of a punitive force can be experienced as the loss of the good object, and its replacement by something altogether different: the harsh authority bent on punishment. The intensely destructive emotions provoked by neglect form into an aggressively destructive internal object relationship in which it is possible for the self to be identified with both roles: the aggressor and his or her victim. In the drama, the self appears as all of the following: the violent outlaw, the equally violent lawman, and the innocent victim.

CHAPTER FIVE

Shame and the Impaired Self

In the story of *Godless*, one character most clearly represents the internalization of the impaired self: Bill McNue, the sheriff of La Belle. Bill's specific (physical) impairment is that he is going blind. He has just returned to La Belle from a vain attempt to find a cure for his blindness using the traditional medicine of a Native American tribe. In an episodic conversation with an old Native American man, Bill speaks of the idea he might find a cure for his blindness as "wishful thinking," saying, "I ain't got none of that in me no more." Visiting his wife Anna's grave, Bill tells her that he is a "failure at just about everything," that his "twilight has come," that he is "useless in the eyes of everyone."

Being unable to see, Bill is unable to protect the people in La Belle from the catastrophe represented by Frank and his gang. In other words, the consequence of his impairment is the inability to keep the innocent safe. The blindness of those on whom we depend is, however, also the defining quality of what we have lost, which is their responsiveness to us, or, using the metaphor of sight, their ability to *see* us. Bill is, then, a complex character in that he represents both the (internalized) parent who fails to respond to and care for us; and, at the same time, the impaired self we discover we have when the responsive parent is unavailable. Bill's failure is internalized as a self-state: shame. Indeed, understood as a fantasy figure, shame is what Bill represents.

In the story of *Godless*, shame serves a purpose, but it does not serve it well. Its purpose is to motivate Bill to do his job, which means to risk his life against overwhelming odds in defense of the people of La Belle. But, because Bill is going blind, no amount of shaming can yield the desired result. This is an important point. The attempt to shame someone does not fix an impaired capacity to care for the self, whether our own or the self-in-other. It leads instead to a kind of despair. As it turns out, the women of La Belle, in whose eyes Bill feels he is not a man, are unaware that he is going blind. Their contempt for him will not keep them safe except in one way: It can, by offering them a target or container for projection of their own shameful selves, protect them from their shame at their inability to protect themselves and their town. Shaming others, while it cannot motivate them to do what they are needed to do, serves the purpose of disavowing our own shame by using others to contain it.

The use of others to contain our shame can be an attack on their impulse to protect themselves from harm. Bill is unavailable to defend La Belle because he is seeking a cure for his blindness. In other words, he is taking care of himself rather than taking care of others. Defining care for the self as a form of cowardice motivates individuals to put themselves at risk in the interest of protecting others from harm. In *Godless*, the problem is meant to be resolved when the women of La Belle mobilize will against fear, risking their lives in defense of themselves and their town.

Norms and Identity

The task of becoming an adult is the task of translating an original vitality into a concrete, particular way of life: from aliveness as an abstract state of being to a specific identity and way of living. Making this translation realizes ideals of living, or, in the language used for social systems, secures the individual's attachment to norms. Norms are ideals of living made real and objective by their ability to connect individuals to the larger society and the ideas that animate it, and are instantiated there. The individual undergoes a gradual transition first into the norms of family life, then into the norms of the larger society, which must be consonant with family norms. Shame can play a more or less powerful role in assuring that this transition succeeds.

Norms become of special importance when we consider the matter of identity. Identity is the form of being and way of life that links the individual to the norms of a larger social order. Identity formation can be a process in which the self plays a vital role. In other words, it can be the process through which the individual achieves self-expression in living. Alternatively, identity can be a way of hiding the self so that it will not be visible to others or known to them. Which path the individual takes—hiding the self or self-expression—depends on the valence of the emotional investment in the self that develops early in life. In other words, the relation both to norms and to identity develops in the context of object relations in which the self has been found either defective (bad) or effective (good).

When the relationship to norms is shaped by object relations in which the self cannot be effective, norms serve the purpose of hiding the self, and shame becomes an essential element in the individual's emotional life. These norms are ways of living defined outside of and against the individual's original vitality. They also serve as a defense against the danger posed, or felt to be posed, by contact with the self, contact that is best avoided if the self is to remain hidden from others, as it must be. Under these conditions, shaping an identity that effectively hides the self is a defense against activating the memory of the experience of loss of psychic or emotional existence in the presence of the primary objects or original caregivers.

Attachment to a group identity, as well as a cultural identity in so far as that is a group identity, can serve this defensive purpose. When it does, the fear of losing cultural identity through the destruction of, or disconnection from, the group is the fear of losing a vital defense against the knowledge that a profound disconnection from the self has already occurred. Fear of losing ties to a cultural group is not, then, fear of loss of being—as in existential anxiety—because, for the group member, being has already been lost. Rather, taking on a group identity is a way of defending against the risk of exposure of the (earlier) loss of the individual's being, his or her original vitality or true self. This use of group identity as a defense parallels the use of attachment to group norms as a defense. Both protect the individual against the awareness or discovery of the loss of emotional or subjective existence.

An important quality of norms is that they are typically experienced by the child as arbitrary in the following sense: What makes behavior that violates norms bad is that the parent says it is bad and often reinforces his or her words with a stern tone and, possibly, with physical restraint or even attack. In other words, certain behaviors are not bad for a reason, nor need reasons for punishment be given; they are bad because the parents declare, through their words and actions, that they are bad. As the child matures, the arbitrary quality of his or her relation to norms may diminish and may be replaced by an understanding of the reasons that inform the norms; or maturation may mean merely learning how to comply with norms to avoid punishment.

The extent to which the arbitrary quality of norms can be superseded by understanding the reasons for them depends on the extent to which the norms instantiate an ideal of autonomy and self-determination. In the language of the metaphor from *Godless*: The development of the capacity to live in accordance with norms can represent either breaking or taming what is wild (the horse) inside (which represents the individual's original vitality). To tame rather than break the horse, you must provide it with a compelling reason to choose or decide to comply. To be sure, the very young child will not know this reason and will only later see how attachment to norms is a vital aspect of self-determination. Still, that quality of the norms can be communicated in the quality of the earliest object relations, especially in the extent to which reasons, on one hand, or physical or emotional violence, on the other, play a predominant role in enforcing norms. Simply put: Taming the horse keeps its vitality alive but reshapes the expression of that vitality to make it consistent with living in the world outside. Breaking the horse destroys its vitality. Breaking the horse is a metaphor for the kind of assault we associate with the use of shame in fostering the transition to living outside the individual's purely subjective, or inner, world.

Norms consistent with self-determination are respected because of their relationship to a good object and to the love of that object. Because the good object represents a safe place to be, compliance expresses trust rather than fear. Then, the shame felt in forcible submission is not the vital element in attachment to norms. Shaming—or breaking the horse—is the alternative to stewardship in parenting. Shaming seeks to activate the individual's connection to his or her defective self in order to secure the hiding of the self and the subordination of conduct to the group.

Limit-setting for children will not lead to the conviction that they have a bad self unless the self is made the target of limit-setting and limit-setting takes the form of harsh discipline or loss of love. It would not be inappropriate, then, to limit the term shame to the more violent and self-negating modalities of discipline. If we consider shame in this way, the link to violence is essential. Shame is experienced when we are unable to defend ourselves against the attempt by others to diminish or destroy our presence of being and independence of thought and movement in order to substitute their agency for ours.

Shame and Adulthood

What it means to be an adult and therefore what is entailed in the maturation process depends on the part self-determination plays in the definition of adulthood. Adulthood may be defined as the exercise of the capacity for autonomous living, in which case maintaining contact with the self in the context of relating to others, including strangers, is essential. Alternatively, adulthood may be defined as internalizing culturally defined norms of living rooted in submerging the individual into the group. Norms of this kind are, in important ways, inconsistent with autonomy. Indeed, maintaining the capacity to make contact with the self may impair the development of the capacity to be an adult, if being an adult means subordination of the self to the group. Then, hiding the self becomes the aim of maturation, and the internalized dynamic of shaming will likely play an important role in achieving this aim. The greater the predominance in society of norms that conflict with self-determination, the more shame will be attached to the urge to care for the self. Then, becoming an adult means suppressing impulses associated with self-determination, and preoccupation with the prospect of being shamed will disable creativity in living in favor of compliance.

We can apply these considerations to the matter of the relationship between shame and morality explored by Martha Nussbaum (2004). The more shame shapes the instantiation of norms, the more powerful the element of violence will be at the core of the social order. Likewise, the more morality is instituted against the ideal of the autonomous self, and the more the idea of a moral order is one of submission to a group-defined way of life, the more intense the violence will be. This intense violence, however, will not be inconsistent with morality in so far as violence expresses the attack on the self that establishes the bond of the individual to the larger society conceived as a group. Indeed, violence of this sort is embedded in morality.

To the extent that being an adult means self-determination, or being your own person, the same factor—shame—that would seem to promote adult behavior also disables the capacity to be an adult. If there is too much emphasis on shame in childhood and too little celebration of the child-person, the adult finds him- or herself in a dilemma. While adulthood is all about being active rather than passive, at the same time it means repressing what, for the child, was the essence of activity: primitive forms of self-expression. In shame-oriented groups and societies, this earlier notion of what it means to be active is replaced with its opposite: Activity means being the agent of self-repression, whether that be the self-in-self or the self-in-other. In settings of this kind, being an adult means using aggression against the impulse to be present, or to exist for -self.

To achieve this end, the method used is the withdrawal of love so that the loss of love will become attached to self-expression. The withdrawal of love in response to self-expression results in the conviction that there is something wrong with the self, so that the doing that emanates out of it is also wrong. When the self is experienced to be wrong in an essential way, the emotional response tied to that experience is anxiety about the destruction or disappearance of the self: the feeling that survival is at risk in a world made dangerous for the self. The loss of access to the self in the inner world makes that world a desolate place dominated by harshly self-destructive internal object relations of the kind discussed in Chapter One in connection with the formation of internal gangs. When shame becomes an attack on the self, it operates along the same lines as the feelings associated with nonexistence, and even contributes to them.

The conviction that the self is intrinsically bad can mimic the badness we associate with guilt. If the group represents the good object, and adherence to group norms represents attachment to the good object, then being-for-self will be defined as an attack on the group and the self will be experienced as bad in a moral sense. Under these circumstances, care for the self is automatically doing harm to others because it represents an attack on the group to which they belong. It therefore violates an important norm. Then, no real distinction exists between guilt and shame. When this happens, the experience of an impaired self—a self about which we might be ashamed—is moved onto the plane of guilt.

Guilt signals taking responsibility for damage done to the good object. Here, we might take note of the way bystanders—those who watch but do nothing as harm is done to the innocent—are shamed for not doing their duty as defined by social role (man or woman for example). This shame can be redefined as guilt (bystander guilt) in order to move the emotional response to failure to prevent violence onto the terrain of personal responsibility rather than shame, which is the terrain on which living up to a norm of adulthood is at issue.

In this instance, the impulse to equate guilt with shame requires that responsibility for damage done to the innocent be somehow attributed to those who do nothing more than stand by. In subsequent chapters we consider this matter more closely. What we will find is that the effort to equate the two tends to obscure what is distinctive to each so that the way guilt binds the individual to society is equated with the way shame attaches individuals to societal norms, especially by obscuring the distinction between societies bound together by group norms and societies bound together by the shared ideal of self-determination. Obscuring this distinction is closely connected to the power of ascribed group identity in social processes.

Shame and the Basic Fault

If to be an adult is to be your own person, then those aspects of identity that are recognized in society as marking you as less than fully a person must be sources of shame. Here, we are thinking about more or less severe forms of denigration of identity and of the imposition of an ascribed identity. What attachment to denigrated identities tells us is that those attached to them are incapable of completing the process of maturation to adulthood and thereby gaining capacity for self-determination associated with being an adult and full participation in adult society. When this interpretation develops, there also develops a connection between shame and the basic fault as the interpretation hinges on the insistence that members of denigrated groups are marked by the presence in them of a flawed self.

Connecting shame to the basic fault expresses the wish that we only feel there is something wrong with us because of a societal norm, in other words, that the basic fault is just a norm and is, therefore, subject to social control. If this were true, we could rid ourselves of our faulty self by being told it is not so, which, of course, means that we have it because we were told by society that something about us, most notably our group identity, is faulty. Our attempt to invest this power in society mirrors the relational quality of the basic fault which develops in a relationship, or more specifically, in the withdrawal of a relationship in which we felt we mattered. But it misconstrues the nature of that relationship to assume that it operated in the same way as the relationship of the adult to societal norms, or, more specifically, that the loss of primary love can be rectified by being told, later in life, that you matter, when no amount of reassurance can substitute for the environment of primary love afforded the young child, an environment that is no longer available.

Denigrated identities are imposed or created by acts of humiliation, especially acts of violence directed at members of groups that affirm that they have no will of their own, that they cannot act on their own initiative, and that they will always live as children in a violent and child-hating family. If this is, indeed, the case because members of these groups are prevented from gaining and exercising adult capacities, especially the capacity for autonomous living, then they will inevitably internalize this deeply problematic sense of who they are. They find themselves in a trap because the self-hate they experience does, in fact, disable, to one degree or another, their capacity to be adults, thus providing an internal validation of the shame imposed from outside.

Given the impairment or disabling of the self as an internal matter, to cope with their predicament, victims of shaming cannot call on *self*-assertion to defend themselves, but, instead, have recourse to their primary assets: an excess of self-hate and the hatred of development to which Bion (1961) draws our attention. It is not surprising, then, to find victims of group oppression using three related strategies. The first is projection, including the use of aggression and violence to project their denigrated selves onto others. The second is insistence that the disabled self, rather than being a source of shame, is a source of pride, so they are fortunate to have it. And the third is the conviction that self-hate can be dispelled by an act of will. After all, parents impose shame on their children through what appears to the child to be an act of will, while at the same time insisting that the capacity to act as an adult is simply a matter of mobilizing will against desire. This is another aspect of the trap of adult activity referred to above.

Shaming affirms and reinforces the individual's conviction that there exists, at the core of his or her personality, a basic fault. Internalization of shame creates a powerful force within the psyche that signals the ever-present danger of shaming and therefore provokes the withdrawal of the self from any interactions that threaten to recall the psychic pain associated with the original experience of the loss of primary love. Because of this, shaming is used by society to enforce attachment to norms consistent with the disconnection of the self from doing and relating. Adherence to such norms defends the individual against awareness of the basic fault, because adherence simultaneously defends against shame. It does not, however, reduce the internal source of shame but, rather, seeks to displace it onto external containers by seeking and finding in others and in most, if not all, social interactions, an intention to humiliate.

The conviction about the presence of a basic fault does not arise because of a too-intense repression of the self or too-intense association of childlike behavior with reprimands and punishments. Rather, it arises out of absence and loss, which is to say a failure of affirming responses to the presence of the self. The result of this is not shame but the feeling of nonexistence and the inability to have an impact in the world. It is futility rather than shame that dominates here: not "I am, or have been, bad," but, "What's the point?" Guilt, of course, has to do not with the prospect that a childlike self will be exposed, but with aggression against a good object. At the same time, the "guilty self" may be experienced as a "bad" self but not because it is and remains immature, but because of a need for repair of an object that cannot be repaired.

The move toward a guilty self, as suggested in James Baldwin's insistence on his responsibility for all harm done, can be understood as a manic defense against the overwhelming sense of futility associated with the basic fault. The more insistent his assertion of responsibility, the more insistent the assertion of agency against the pressure of an inner or unconscious conviction that he has none, that there is nothing he can do. What sounds like a response to the cry for help of those who suffer is, in reality, his own cry for help in gaining his freedom from the imprisonment of the self and the feeling of despair associated with it.

If norms represent internalization of the good object as an ideal, failure to live up to norms can be a hate phenomenon: hatred of norms equals hatred of the good object. Now the failure of guilt to restrict conduct is also a failure of shame; both indicate a weak attachment to the good. Then, the two terms get confused. But shamelessness, unlike remorselessness, can be considered acceptable, even good, when norms are restrictive in unnecessary or assaultive ways.

Shaming as a Virtue

If we approach the ideas of the destroyed world, guilt, and shame in the way suggested above, we may find curious the number of prominent political, legal, and ethical theorists who have advocated political norms, criminal punishments, and other forms of censure designed specifically to recall, to affected individuals and groups, experiences of inner, psychic destruction. What is more, these scholars have done so in the name of tempering or eliminating destructive forces in society and protecting the world from harm. In such advocacies, we witness, once again, the operation of fantasies about guilt and shame that resonate in important ways with ideologies and philosophies, discussed in the Introduction, that emphasize the destructive force of the self. Here, the fantasy is that shamed and shameful selves cannot do harm, that the psychic destruction wrought in them by shame will prevent them from wreaking havoc in the world outside.

Contemporary advocates of the political and moral virtues of shame, such as Kahan (1996, 2006), Etzioni (1999), Tarnopolsky (2010), and Deonna, Rodogno, and Teroni (2012), argue that shame can produce a democratic ethos of self-limitation, self-regulation, and a consensual rejection of shameless conduct. Their accounts rely on explicit fears of social degeneration that seem, at the same time, to reflect unconscious anxieties about the destruction of the inner world. That is, we might say that, for shame to be seen as a virtue, the contours of a destroyed world have to be internalized, such that the possibility of destruction seems best averted by derogating, humiliating, and repressing selves, since it is the activity of the self that is presumed to be inherently bad and threatening.

Those who have endorsed shaming specifically as a criminal punishment and public ethos, such as Etzioni (1999) and Kahan (especially in his early work on the subject), base their endorsement on a way of thinking about the relationship between the internal dynamics of the self, the impulses set in motion there, and acts that do damage to others. Consider, for example, Tarnopolsky, who asks: "Don't we wish that people like Hitler or Eichmann had felt ashamed of their treatment of Jews, Gypsies, and gays?" (2010, p. 2), the implication being that had they felt shame they would have treated their chosen victims differently. Tarnopolsky's question is, of course, posed rhetorically and therefore is meant to contain its answer. But if, instead, we consider it a real question to which the answer is not clear a priori but depends on making explicit an understanding of internal dynamics of shame and self-hate outlined above, it might be possible to approach an answer to the question that is not presupposed in its formulation.

A starting point might be the way people manage the presence in the psyche of destructive attacks on the positive investment in the self.

Typically, efforts to manage a damaged or denigrated self involve two processes. The first is withdrawal from engagement to protect the self from the possibility of exposure. The second involves the use of aggression to transfer self-hate onto others. It is this second process that theorists insist can be preempted or circumvented by shame. The problem, of course, is that shaming activates self-hate, so that rather than preempting the violence involved in the effort to relieve the psyche of the pain of self-hate, shaming promotes violence, or, more precisely, is an act of violence.

It cannot, then, be assumed that shame was not in play in prompting the horrific attacks on the integrity of others we associate with Hitler and Eichmann, especially when we consider that their conduct fits well with the second response to self-hate indicated above. Then, we cannot avoid the possibility that self-hate of the kind typically associated with shame was implicated in their conduct, which likely involved an effort to rid themselves of intolerable feelings about themselves by transferring them, through violence, onto others. Not feeling the presence in themselves of an impaired self was exactly the point of their aggression against others. So, to the extent that this transfer process succeeded, it would be true to say that they did not feel that their selves were unworthy. But it would also follow that the more we attempt to impose shame on them, the more intense would be their need to externalize their impaired selves through violent acts.

So far as our end is to replace aggression against others with concern and empathy, our problem is to understand the relationship between intense states of self-hate, such as those sometimes associated with shame, and the capacity for empathy. Here, it is important to note how self-hate is the enemy of empathy, how the experience of self-destruction entailed by self-hate does not create empathy. Rather, it either creates diffidence or empowers the impulse to redirect aggression away from the self and towards others. Insistence that experiencing self-destruction creates empathy for others involves us in a kind of fantasy whereby we reimagine the destructive impulse as its opposite, we redefine vice as virtue, which is, of course, something we are more inclined to do the more the vice resides in ourselves. We can see this most clearly if we bear in mind that shaming, as an act of violence, involves us in the same kind of activity we insist it is our purpose to preempt.

It may be the case that enthusiasm for shame as a political virtue relies on a misunderstanding of shame that elides traditional distinctions between guilt and shame. Most argue or imply that shame holds the same virtue as guilt, which amounts to a kind of remorseful and cautious posture in which the self's presence, intentions, and activities (past, present, and future) are considered, first, in terms of the self's tendency to do harm (see e.g. Tarnopolsky 2010, pp. 31, 93). Sometimes referred to as "democratic shame," such accounts err in ways similar to calls for "democratic mourning," which often amount to demands for a collective melancholia linking the experience of shame not to any qualities possessed by the individual but, via a normative injunction imposed by a group or community, to the conviction that the presence of the self within the group or community is potentially destructive.

Just as guilt serves the purpose of creating responsibility and therefore also the possibility of rectification, shame, because it is intended to make our self-state dependent on the way others see us, also places us under their control and, in this sense, expresses the hope that control over the inner world can be exercised in the interest of shaping the way we relate to others. So far as the self-state over which we wish we could exercise control is the one associated with impairment of the self (basic fault), placing the matter onto the terrain of shame expresses the wish that we could also take control, via participation in a social defense, of our basic fault. But, wishing does not make it so, and the basic fault persists. Indeed, our conviction that there is something intrinsically wrong with us is reinforced by its use for societal ends through making the threat of activating that conviction by shaming an ever-present danger of living in society and in groups. The greater the role of shame in social relations, the greater the danger posed by the prospect of exposure of the reality of the impaired self, the more families are organized around rejection and abandonment of the self, the more abandonment becomes a norm. Shame, then, is simply a social device for perpetuating the damage to the self we have referred to in the language of the basic fault.

Consider, in this connection, Abdel-Nour's discussion of the virtue of shame in defending the group.

> In Augustin's terms, shame collapses the sinner with the sin. It tends to focus the agent's attention on *who she is*. The hope … is that her shame can be an occasion for the agent to grow and develop and "to become a person that is not shameful." For the only way to get rid of shame is to change oneself … When a mature agent … discovers that the founding of the strong, stable union came at the heavy price of legitimating the institution of slavery for more than half a century, such a person is not led to an admission of guilt (that would be disingenuous, since she would do

> it again). Rather, she might be led to reflect on the kind of person she is, at what it says about her to be proud of this act of founding … The agent who participates in this form of belonging incurs a responsibility for that part of herself that is caught up in the nation. This responsibility she incurs by means of her national identity alone. In practical terms this means that her birth after the abolition of slavery, the extermination or expulsion of native populations, or any other horror in the nation's past does not in itself *necessarily* absolve her of all responsibility for these horrors … The agent can implicate herself with the causes of these horrors via her imagination. (2003, pp. 709-713, *emphasis in original*)

Here, an agent becomes responsible for the horrors of slavery simply by imagining them. Or, more precisely, the degree to which an agent is responsible depends on *how* that agent imagines destruction and to what degree he or she internalizes guilt and self-hatred as a part of that imagining. Responsibility for the very real destruction of persons, groups, and cultures is laid at the feet of all who belong to or participate in—as we all must—groups, communities, and nations connected to that destruction. In this way, valorizations of shame and self-disruption entrench destroyed-world fantasies and all they entail, rather than protecting individuals and groups from real or imagined destruction.

CHAPTER SIX

Speaking Out, Remaining Silent

Participation

A long-standing theme in democratic society is the obligation to participate, sometimes expressed as a moral indictment of those who do not. Part of the issue centers on the matter of the size and scope of modern polities, a size and scope that tend to undermine any conviction that what the individual does or says matters. Indeed, it could be said that part of the intensity of the call to involvement stems from the fear that, for the reason just mentioned, participation does not, in fact, matter. To the extent that this is the case, the moral imperative to participate becomes a defense against the anxiety associated with knowing that what we do and say, and therefore who we are, does not matter.

A comparable dynamic operates on the terrain of the struggle over speaking out and remaining silent. It is not, after all, only with respect to voting that acting can express the conviction that who we are and what we do matters. Indeed, failure to speak can be taken to express our conviction that what we have to say does not matter, whereas speaking out is a way of insisting that it does. Going a step further, our failure to speak out can be taken as a challenge to others if it is experienced by them as casting doubt on whether they matter, reinforcing the anxiety against which the moral imperative to speak out is meant to defend them.

The issue of acting and speaking, or failing to do so, can be formulated in the language of activity and passivity. In that language, the defense to which we have just referred is a defense against passivity and those qualities related to it: apathy, dependence, compliance, docility, cowardice. One way to think about the attack on silence embodied, for example, in the slogan, "silence is violence," is that it is an expression of the struggle over passivity. Indeed, in many cases, activity is best understood not as an emanation of initiative, agency, or what is active or vital in the self but, rather, as a defense against fears of being—or being seen as, or seeing oneself as—passive, along with whatever that entails. The struggle over passivity can be a struggle against loss of existence, which may be experienced as something imposed from outside (victimization) or taken to reflect an original deficit or fault within the self.

Speaking Out

An account of a personal experience offered by Danielle Johnson, resident director at Bridgewater State University, can help us gain some insight into the struggle over silence and the moral imperative to speak out (Johnson, 2016). While visiting her family one weekend, Johnson found herself listening in on a discussion between a grandfather and three boys, none of whom she knew prior to that weekend. She describes the incident in the following way:

> As I was sitting there enjoying the book I was reading, the grandfather and the three boys were playing in and near the water. The second oldest boy obviously didn't want to go in all the way, and was standing by the water's edge. I then heard what the grandfather was saying to try to get him in. "C'mon, *girl*." The grandfather goaded the boy. "Get in the water, *girl*." It was very clear by his tone of voice that calling the boy a "girl" was meant to be an insult and he would stop calling him that once he got into the water.

In response to observing this incident, Johnson felt she had two options. She could remain silent and thereby avoid offending anyone. Or, she could "choose to say something to the grandfather and then subsequently make a scene." In the end, she "chose to say nothing. But once the moment had passed, [she] realized that [she] had done some serious damage by not speaking out."

What was this "serious damage?" To Johnson's way of thinking, by leaving the grandfather's statement standing without challenge, she left his words in control of what the boy would grow up believing, which is "that being a girl is the worst thing that you can be." This suggests, among other things, that Johnson believes she holds real and significant power over the man this boy will grow up to be. Because Johnson holds that power, being privy to this encounter makes her responsible for the result of the boy's growing-up experience. She holds this responsibility whether she speaks out or remains silent, although the result for the boy would differ radically. In adopting this stance, Johnson participates in a larger public concern organized around notions such as "bystander guilt" and the importance of "speaking out."

It is worth considering more closely the idea that being a girl is "the worst thing you can be." Johnson does not tell us what this means precisely; we do not know along what dimension "the worst" is defined, nor what makes being a girl so bad. But her language clearly suggests an extreme interpretation of the harm being done in the scene to which she is a witness. If we consider her experience in the context of the issues with which we are concerned here, it would not be unreasonable to think about her statement as an indication of the presence in her of a concern about her gender and the possibility that it marks her as defective in some basic way, indeed, in the most basic way. This would be consistent with the connection between shame and the basic fault considered in Chapter Five, and, as we will see, this interpretation gains some support from a closer consideration of what she has to say about her encounter.

The idea that those who fail to speak out in the presence of violence are responsible for the violence they fail to prevent has deeply rooted emotional drivers including: (1) the insistence that the bad things that happen to people must be preventable, which is the other side of experiencing helplessness in the face of assault as intolerable, and (2) the need to externalize guilt feelings associated with violent attacks on those who are innocent and helpless. In other words, insistence on the guilt of bystanders stems from deeply held beliefs and complex feelings about innocence, guilt, and helplessness. So far as this is correct, we can trace the idea of bystander guilt to early experiences encoded in memory-inspired fantasies, or, in other words, fantasies constructed to correct for those aspects of memories that cannot be tolerated, such as the memory of doing nothing when action was called for.

This connection of the imperative to speak out to early experience is well expressed by Johnson when, in the aftermath of the events described in her article, she chastises herself because she "chose to be comfortable instead of speaking up for [herself] and for women everywhere." She "allowed a moment to happen that continued the cycle of [her] own oppression and the oppression of women everywhere, and a moment that hurt men and masculinity too." By linking the experience at the family weekend to her own oppression, she suggests how it activated a memory. When Johnson refers to a "cycle" of her own oppression, she is necessarily speaking about her own history, about things that happened in her past. By exploring her commentary on her contemporary experience, we can begin to identify not only her memory of past experience, but also the fantasy embedded in that memory.

Johnson chose her own comfort over speaking out because she felt that to speak out would be to put herself at risk. She feared an angry and violent (at least verbally violent) response. So, she remained silent to protect herself; but she did so at the cost of putting women at risk of becoming future victims of a boy on his way to becoming the kind of man who does not treat women with respect. We may even say that Johnson holds herself responsible for her failure to transform the boy into a man who will not be a destructive force in the world.

This is a striking response on Johnson's part. In it, she takes responsibility for something over which it can reasonably be said she has no control: the relationship between a stranger and his grandchild. Why does she do so? Why does she think she holds the power and, therefore, has the responsibility she ascribes to herself? Why does she think there are words she could have spoken that would have changed the trajectory of the boy's life and, with it, the lives of those with whom the boy will interact? Put in the language used above: Why does she believe that what she says or does not say in this setting *matters*?

Johnson's own answer to these questions is that she thinks she has both the power and the responsibility to speak out because she rejects the idea that the words we use have limited impact, even in the setting she describes. Johnson teaches her students that people "don't want to believe that [words] have that much impact. But everyone's voice matters." People do not believe that speaking up will have any effect, but they may be wrong. "I could have said something and the boy could have grown up believing all the wrong things about women anyway," Johnson explains, "but we'll never know, because I didn't even try." This last is also, in its way, an odd statement, since, whether she tried or not, we are unlikely to know the effect of her intervention on the trajectory of the boy's life, so far as knowing that trajectory is a matter of finding out what sort of man the boy will grow up to be.

This observation suggests that knowledge about the outcome of interventions such as the one Johnson contemplated after the fact must have a source different from any empirical study of the individual who is or is not the subject of an intervention. What sort of knowledge might this be? Clearly, we are dealing with knowledge about the impact of words on the individual's life and, especially, the orientation toward others he or she takes later in life. On this matter, Johnson provides little guidance. There is, however, one possibility consistent with Johnson's account, which is that, for knowledge about the impact of words on emotional development, she calls on the one case with which she is intimately familiar: her own. In other words, we need to consider the possibility that Johnson's assessment of the potential impact of her words on the boy is shaped primarily by projection of her own experience of the power of words over her. In this sense, it is not the trajectory of the boy's life with which she is concerned, but of her own.

It is not unusual for the power attributed to speaking out to be understood as derived from the power of words to alter something important about the way people think about themselves, about others, and about the way they relate to one another. To be sure, in one sense, the power of speaking must be the power to use words to affect something important in the world. Still, it does not follow that the power of speaking must reside in the words spoken taken by themselves, which is to say: separate from the person speaking and the significance attributed to that person. Yet, it is this separation to which Johnson implicitly appeals. Otherwise, how could words spoken to a stranger have power to alter the way that stranger views and relates to women?

Still, it is reasonable to assume that whether the words spoken have the power Johnson attributes to them depends on who is speaking those words, and, more specifically, on the significance that person has for those listening. What is interesting in Johnson's account is that she invests so much significance in what she, a stranger, might have said. Put another way, she ignores the importance of relationship in determining the power of words. That she does so becomes clear if we consider the impact of the grandfather's words more closely.

So far as Johnson is concerned, the grandfather's abusive language was directed at women. Women were not, however, the primary target of the abuse she observed that day. Rather, the victim of the grandfather's abuse was his grandson. Yet, Johnson nowhere objects to the way the grandfather treated the boy, his intent to disparage and humiliate him. Rather, she objects only because the language used to humiliate the boy expressed a disparaging attitude toward women. Nowhere in her narrative did she express empathy or concern for the boy. In this sense, the aggressive impulse she felt toward the grandfather (and perhaps also toward the man the boy would become) but suppressed was not mobilized to protect the person being abused. It could even be said that speaking out against the grandfather's disparaging comment about women, had she done so, could be considered a way of remaining silent about his abuse of his grandson. Then, by her own standard, according to which failing to speak out against acts of violence makes us responsible for them, she would have been guilty of a violent act against the grandson.

Why was she unable to hear the abuse of the boy but able to hear the grandfather's abusive attitude toward women? One answer involves her need to reject her own passivity. Empathy with the boy would mean empathy with the passive, abused self he represented. It would therefore require identification with the boy, and therefore with her passive self contained in him, whereas her entire account suggests her struggle against her passive self and her identification with it. Thus, in her narrative, we see Johnson struggling simultaneously with her identification with the victim and with her rejection of any suggestion that such an identification might exist.

Another answer to the question, "Why did Johnson fail to hear the abuse of the child?" suggests itself if we consider the way her experience that day came to be subsumed into her fantasies, particularly her fantasy constructs of men and women. If, in those fantasy constructs, men are inherently abusive and women are always targets of their abuse, then it would not be surprising to find her unable to see abuse directed toward the party in a relationship who is not, or who will not become, a woman. To be sure, her insistence that an intervention on her part might stop the development of the boy into a man who abuses women suggests that this mapping of abuser and abused onto men and women might not be inevitable. Even so, her suggestion does not preclude the operation of an equation between men and abusers, especially at the unconscious level.

Because it engages fantasy narratives and fantasy figures, albeit represented in real persons, Johnson's struggle is an internal one. What she describes as a failure to intervene into a present-day interaction between two strangers became a fantasized failure to intervene in a fantasized event. Fantasy is one way we remember and invest meaning in events that have already occurred, especially during our growing-up experiences. When shaped by fantasy, we experience the present-day event as if it were the older experience transferred into the present and onto surrogate actors (in Johnson's case, the boy and his grandfather). These may be older experiences in which we remained silent in the face of humiliation, degradation, or abuse, accepting or internalizing a shameful self. The shameful self is the self that remains silent (passive) in the face of abuse, which is not only what Johnson confesses to have done but what the boy did in his interaction with his grandfather. Or, they can be older experiences in which we spoke out, but in so doing provoked aggression against us from an adult who was much more powerful than we were. In either case, like Johnson, we experience the words spoken as triggers or provocations to identify with a character in an internal drama. If we understand Johnson's experience in this way, we can begin to understand the power that words have for her. Words have power because they can activate fantasies, or internal object relations, and the emotions associated with them.

Confusion of internal (fantasy) objects with persons in the world outside not only causes emotional suffering, it also fosters the hope that, by changing the external object, we can alter the terms of the internal object relation. And, because of the way words act as triggers, and can do damage by acting that way, the construction of the situation based on hope fosters the conviction that we can free ourselves from the terms of the fantasy if we can prevent the words from being spoken, the trigger from being pulled. This conviction is, however, part of the fantasy and not a real path to overcome our identification with victims of abuse. Indeed, the idea of words as triggers is part of a fantasy about the origins of abuse and the way we can escape from it. That is, Johnson equates the words with the abuse primarily because, by activating her identification with a character in an internal drama, words provoke her to experience once again the abuse suffered in the relationship called to mind. But, if the source of suffering lies in the internalized relationship, embedded in fantasy, then blocking the words that trigger the fantasy leaves the fantasy, and with it the source of suffering, intact.

An early experience in which we remained silent in the face of abuse, especially when it was part of an ongoing and emotionally important relationship, can become a recurring fantasy (or internal object relation) in which the individual attempts to purge powerful feelings of shame by fixing the fantasized interaction so that in it, rather than remaining silent, we speak out, thereby releasing ourselves from the prison of our shame. This is essentially what Johnson attempts to do: turn a fantasy of humiliation into its opposite by imagining herself speaking out in a present-day encounter with a person in the outside world.

If, in her response to the present-day event, Johnson repeated her passivity by remaining silent in the face of what she saw as a repetition of an earlier experience, in her internal response to that repetition subsequent to the event, she sought to fix what she had done (or not done) by imagining that she *had* spoken out, just as she imagined a future in which speaking out is what she will do. To the extent that this interpretation is correct, and the boy represents her passive or silent self, Johnson's wish-invested narrative about altering the past and doing better in the future is a fantasy in which she severs her identification with the boy, both by denying that his abuse happened—by remaining silent about it—and by rebuking the grandfather for his disparaging attitude toward women. Doing so suggests not only her refusal to acknowledge her identification with the victim, but, through her act of silence, her identification with the aggressor.

Johnson constructs a set of fantasies of the future: of speaking out and becoming the victim of a violent response, of the boy growing up to be a misogynist because she does not speak out, and of his growing up to be the kind of man who respects women because she does. She also activates the all-important fantasies (1) of her failing to speak out and becoming ever after the victim of her own harshly negative judgment of herself, and (2) of her speaking out and becoming a courageous, even heroic, self, thereby neutralizing that harsh self-judgment. Among these possible consequences, the most important and predictable is the one in which her failure to speak out provokes her identification with a shameful self and the perpetuation of a humiliating internal object relationship into the future. It is the most important and predictable because, by her own admission, it actually occurred. It is the consequence of silence that, for someone in Johnson's position, is most clearly and unavoidably linked to it. Put another way, the harm assured to follow from silence is not the harm to the boy, or the harm to women in the future resulting from what the boy might become, but the harm she does to herself.

The complex emotional situation in which Johnson found herself is by no means unique to her. On the contrary, we can assume that, although its form and intensity may vary from person to person, its presence is more or less universal. Without dismissing the gender concerns expressed in Johnson's version of the dilemma in which she found herself, we can still understand her problem not only as a gender issue, but also as the internalization of a primitive object relation organized around shame. Her struggle over speaking out or remaining silent enacts the internalized relationship in all its complexity. It also highlights the way present-day relationships can be used in an attempt to fix internalized object relations and thereby free the individual from feelings of shame that endure long after the real interactions that shaped the internalized relationship have ceased to be active. Here, "speaking out" is understood to be the way we can fix internal object relations (the endlessly repeated fantasy dialogues through which we call to mind our past humiliations), while remaining silent is the way we express our inability to break free of those relations.

As it turns out, the method for fixing the old (internalized) relationship reproduces that relationship, albeit with the roles reversed. The old relationship is fixed only because the individual finds his or her ability to "speak out," so that the relationship is reversed, and the individual now occupies the active role in it. For the individual to occupy the active role, there must be a present-day occupant of the passive role: the target of aggression. On the surface, this new occupant of the passive role is, or would have been, for Johnson, the grandfather, toward whom Johnson's words of rebuke would have been directed. But, under the surface and outside of awareness, the real occupant of that role is not the grandfather but the boy. To the extent that the boy represents Johnson's victimized, or passive, self, the revised version of the fantasy in which shame is lifted continues to reenact the older version, fixing nothing. The grandfather still abuses the boy, the difference being that he does so using something other than the language of gender. Johnson's passive self remains victimized. The only difference is that, now, her victimization would be more deeply hidden, making the prospect of resolving her dilemma even more remote. The more she acts as victimizer both in her internal drama and in enactments of that drama in present-day relating, the greater the role played by the power of shame in shaping her life.

This result is most apparent in the broader significance the attack on silence has taken on in the struggle over oppression. Once silence is considered an act of violence, aggression directed against those who would remain silent becomes justifiable because it is used to protect the victims.

This makes the attack on those who remain silent a legitimized (morally defensible) way for those who attack them to act out their identification with the aggressor, and thus to be the victimizer, because the target is no longer "the oppressed" but the "oppressor," or, more accurately, both. For Johnson, the boy, who is the victim of abuse, is the container of a future abuser, rather than a victim of abuse. This justifies her in remaining silent about his abuse. Thus, the accusation that "silence is violence" is the acting out of an attack on victims, displaced onto those bystanders who would set themselves outside the drama of victim/victimization.

Those who insist that silence is violence can hear nothing in silence other than a provocation to enact a powerfully invested internal drama of aggression/passivity, victim/victimizer. The more powerful the impulse to construct relationships through projection of bad objects, the more silence will be experienced as a form of aggression, as the silence will be filled with (bad, victimizing) fantasy objects and fantasy relationships.

Silence, Risk, and Withdrawal

What seems to have gotten Johnson into trouble during her family weekend was that, facing the real-time presence of an aggressive and abusive object, or an object assumed to be aggressive and abusive, she exercised an option unavailable to her early in life: She held herself outside any engagement with that object. Her problem was that the strategy she used to do so replicated the passivity that marked her engagement with the earlier objects in her life and expressed her fearful response to the expectation created by early object relations that speaking out would provoke aggression in others. In other words, to stay out of a relationship with a potentially abusive object, she placed herself in what appeared to be the passive role: She remained silent.

To be sure, she experienced her silence as an act of cowardice, which is to say she experienced her fear of the abuser not as a self-protective emotional signal, but as a defect in her moral character. This also means that she identified moral character with engagement with the aggressor. Because of this, her effort to protect herself failed. It failed not because it was an inherently bad strategy, but because she had internalized the terms of the abusive relationship according to which passivity (silence) indicated weakness. As a result, by attempting to protect herself from harm, she ended up harming herself. She harmed herself because she defined self-protection as cowardice, and, as a result, brought shame on herself by withdrawing from an encounter that she feared would put her at risk.

Risk was central to her emotional response to her encounter. Were she to respond to the grandfather's disparaging comment, she would risk becoming the target of his aggression. But the drama she had witnessed was also about risk. In it, the boy faced two risks: (1) the risk of (imagined or real) physical harm associated with going into the water, and (2) the risk of the emotional injury of being shamed for refusing to do so. In a sense, the emotional dilemma Johnson experienced watching the drama was also the dilemma being played out in the drama.

A drama about taking risks is also a drama about courage, or the lack thereof. And because of the grandfather's choice of words, the drama about courage was also a drama about gender identity in which one gender was identified with courage, the other with the lack of courage. Here, courage meant the ability to put yourself at risk. After all, the pejorative use of the term "girl" would be an ineffective threat were it not for what being a "girl" stood for: being someone who was afraid to put him- or herself at risk.

There are times in life when the individual needs to call on the ability to take risks. It is not clear, however, that Johnson was observing such a time in the life of the young boy, or experiencing such a moment in her own. What she was experiencing, especially for the boy, was his grandfather goading him to take a risk for its own sake, to take a risk simply to prove that he could. In other words, his grandfather was playing a game of dare with him, a game in which what was important was to do what someone dared you to do simply because they dared you to do it. It was a test of courage taken as a willingness to risk harm for the sake of proving he was unafraid of doing so.

In her parallel process, Johnson was testing herself in the same way the boy was being tested. In this respect, she was closely identified with the boy who had to do what he feared to do so he would not become a girl. Johnson, too, had to do, or felt she had to do, what she feared to do in order not to discover that being a girl was evidence of the absence of courage. In other words, she faced a test whose outcome would prove she both was and was not a girl. What was unacceptable was to refuse the test.

Games of dare are meant to mobilize the power of will against emotion. Such games, then, have a more general significance as enactments of the power of will. In the gendered version of this enactment, being a girl (or woman) is equated with the power of emotion over will, whereas being a boy or a man is equated with the power of will over emotion. Why does this struggle have so much resonance and why do the stakes seem so high? The answer, to which we have already alluded, is the involvement of shame in the struggle. Under these circumstances, the struggle between will and emotion is a struggle over who will bear the burden of shame, which expresses how vitally important it is to believe that, if we are strong enough, we can rid ourselves of shame by an act of will, in this case by the act of speaking out.

The centrality of shame indicates that what is at stake in the test of will is the worth invested in the self. And yet, the test of will demonstrates the worthiness of the self in a complex and problematic way. If the test of will is one in which we must put ourselves at risk, then we measure the worth of our selves by the disregard with which we treat our selves. We put ourselves at risk to prove that our selves are not weak, and we prove they are not weak by demonstrating our willingness to endanger, damage, or sacrifice them. Our goal is to prove to others that we are not weak. But, underlying that goal is the goal of proving our strength *to ourselves*. We only need to prove our strength to ourselves if the matter of our strength or weakness is in doubt. Thus, it is really our doubt that we have a worthy self that drives us to put ourselves at risk. Our starting point, then, is the fragility of the sense of worth or value in the self, the conviction, however unconscious, that the self is not strong enough to support the weight it must bear.

Putting the self at risk can become a ritualized enactment designed to demonstrate the strength, indeed the invulnerability, of the self. So far as we are convinced that the only self worth having is one that is invulnerable, it is better to risk its destruction than to live with its vulnerability. From this vantage point, a "girl"—in the context discussed here—is, indeed, the worst thing that you can be, if it means accepting the vulnerability of the self. Any effort to protect the self from harm is evidence of vulnerability and, paradoxically, this very effort proves that the self is not worth protecting. This is the same theme we encountered in our discussion in Chapter One of the outlaw gang and the retreat of the self into a psychic fortress. The result is the dilemma experienced by Johnson and depicted in her narrative of the interaction between the boy and his grandfather.

The demand that we must speak out is a demand that we must put ourselves at risk to prove that we are of value. Johnson, it would appear, felt this demand acutely, not only as one originating outside, but also internally. The harsh self-judgment that followed from her failure to speak out indicates how negative is her assessment of herself and how harshly she judges her own actions and inactions aimed at protecting her from harm.

Johnson's internal object relations prevented her from an important emotional experience: the experience of (safely) withdrawing from a threat. This withdrawal may not be the only meaning silence has for her, but it is clearly a primary meaning: Silence and the protection of the self that silence affords, because it invites a harsh self-judgment, promotes shame. Speaking out can prevent shame from making its presence known, but the price of doing so is loss of contact with the self. This is because, while speaking out may be speaking for the self, and therefore expressing the presence of the self, this is not inevitably the case. As we have suggested, speaking out may be an indicator of the intensity of the need to mobilize will against our emotional center and to repress self-experience, which is the experience of the investment of meaning in who we are and what we do. When speaking out is an effort to dispel the perception, on the part of self and others, that our selves are weak, we can be said to speak out *against* rather than *for* the self.

In the case with which we are concerned here, speaking out is a way of injecting ourselves into relationships, including relationships in which we do not belong. It is a way of insisting that there is nothing from which we are excluded. Yet, it is in our inability to withdraw from—to remain outside of and therefore to protect ourselves from—relating that our early object relations are able to exert their continuing power over us, especially by assuring that shame plays a prominent part in our inner landscape. This is the essential point of Johnson's narrative. Her insistence that she must speak out was also her insistence that she must not withdraw from an abusive relationship. She must always be there, in the role of victim, of aggressor, or of both. What is key is her inability to protect herself from relating (on protecting the self from relating, see Winnicott, 1962).

The insistence that "silence is violence" can be understood, in part at least, as an effort to deprive people of a vital method for protecting themselves from external assaults on the self by activating a powerful internal prohibition against withdrawal, one born of a moral imperative associated with membership in groups that insist on the importance of speaking out. Groups of those who must always speak out are made up of those dependent on the defense against shame summarized above. For such groups, silence is an attack on members' (and the groups') moral standing. So far as the individual can hold onto a positive investment in the self without participating in an enactment of the fantasy of the kind expressed in Johnson's narrative, the individual can also live outside the group.

Or, more precisely, the individual can live with him- or herself, rather than within the collective. Then, in a very real sense, the individual can decide for him- or herself whether to engage or withdraw from relating, whether to speak out or remain silent. And, this decision can be made, in part at least, on the basis of its consequences for the need to keep the self secure.

For the group member, however, this decision has already been made by the imperatives of group membership, which treat the ability to remain silent as an attack on the moral necessity of the group. Our ability to decide to remain silent indicates that we can make a positive investment in our selves independently of the group's judgment. This ability takes from the group its authority to adjudicate our moral standing. It denies the necessity that we always "give voice" to the group's beliefs, ideals, and fantasies and that we prevent any voice that challenges the group's beliefs, ideals, and fantasies from speaking.

It is not surprising that, for groups of those who speak out, silence is understood as an attack. After all, from the perspective of such groups, silence *is* violence: a destructive attack on the importance and authority of the group. The presence of group fantasies along this line is clearly evinced in the way Johnson insists that, by speaking out, she would be speaking for (all) women, and that, in so doing, she would be announcing her membership in and putting herself at risk on behalf of the group designated by that term.

The issue of making contact with the self is central to the whole matter of the relationship of the individual to silence. For Johnson, the consequence of remaining silent was that she was unable to tolerate contact with her self because her self had been proven unworthy of respect. The alternative to living with her self was to do what must be done to gain the respect of the group of those who speak out, something she could only do by putting herself at risk. What Johnson could not do was live with herself, or tolerate the person she would become, if she failed to participate in the enactment of a group fantasy. But, to participate in that enactment also meant not making contact with her self because it meant forsaking the possibility of withdrawal from relating, existing outside the group (and its fantasies) in a space where withdrawal is not equated with cowardice and where contact with the self is possible.

Whether we consider silence to be violence or not, silence plays an important role in shaping relationships. Silence in a relationship can be experienced as a failure to respond, and in that sense as a refusal to relate. Regarding Danielle Johnson, it could be said that her emotional reaction to her own silence was, among other things, a rebellion against the way she allowed herself to be excluded from a relationship and her way of managing her exclusion through her fantasized involvement in it. To be excluded from a relationship is to be denied attention and to experience the damaging consequences of that denial.

Exclusion takes on importance because of the kind of relationship from which we are excluded. In this case, what is key is not simply that the parties to the relationship are boys and men, but, rather, that there is (presumed to be) a special meaning invested in relationships between boys and men, fathers and sons. All the information we have about the meaning relationships of this kind have for Johnson is the vignette she offers, involving the grandfather and grandson. In that vignette, the relationship from which Johnson has been excluded is one in which the self exists and is recognized primarily (if not exclusively) to the extent that the individual is able and willing to put himself at risk, a relationship that teaches a lesson about "daring to." As much as Johnson and her readers might resist this interpretation, it is suggested by the way she treats her experience and by the way she (1) does not take note of or object to the way the grandfather treats the boy, and (2) the way she focuses on how the term "girl" is used in the interaction, which is to make the statement: "Girls" are to be excluded from the lesson being taught that day. This suggests the possibility that speaking out is all about forcing herself into a relationship from which she has been excluded, and, not coincidentally, a relationship that is all about having the courage to impose your will on self and others.

The Silent Analyst

Since our concern here is with the meaning of silence and the kind of relationship shaped by silence, it can prove helpful to consider a special relationship in which silence plays an important role: the relationship with the "silent analyst." A significant component of that relationship is the experience of a patient speaking and an analyst listening while remaining silent. By remaining silent, the analyst creates space for the patient to speak or to remain silent, according to the imperatives of a process internal to the patient. During these periods, silence not only creates space for an internal process, but also makes that process available for a special kind of observation, or listening (Bollas, 1987, pp. 236-241; Racker, 1968; Stein, 2017). The silent analyst listens attentively, but in a special sense of the term that emphasizes the availability to the listener of thoughts and associations not created through thinking or interpretation, but through a process of "free floating" or "evenly hovering" attention.

For our purposes, what is vital here is the matter of attentiveness and the way attentiveness shapes a relationship. There is a sense in which the greater the attentiveness of the analyst, the less what is shaped by it is a relationship, in the usual sense of the word. What this means is that a certain kind of attention to the patient lessens the presence of the analyst as someone to whose needs attention must be paid. The purpose of attentiveness in analysis is to assure that relating is all about the patient and not about the needs—including the need to shape relating—of the analyst. Thus, attention may be considered a means of facilitating the patient's *being present* in the relationship in that the patient feels (and is) present because of the attention being paid to him or her.

Yet, while it may be argued that the analyst does what she can to take herself out of the relationship with the patient, it does not follow that the same holds for the patient, who, because he invests the analyst with significant power over his emotional state—including especially the power to create or relieve suffering—finds himself very much in a relationship. Indeed, this investment in another with power over our emotional state is one aspect of what it means to relate.

To relate to others is not necessarily the same as to be in a relationship with them. When we relate, we may have ends ill-served by investing others with the kind of emotional significance implied by an enduring relationship. Being in a relationship with another person is a complicated matter, but includes, at a minimum, the significant and enduring involvement of the other person in the narratives of our fantasy life. The specific role the person occupies in fantasy defines the meaning that person has for us. Words spoken by someone having this kind of involvement in our internal object worlds carry a special importance that those same words, taken outside any such involvement, do not.

It can be argued, of course, that all involvement with other persons has the potential to trigger our impulse to subsume them into fantasy. But, even if this is the case, it does not follow that the degree and intensity of that involvement is always the same, or that there is never room for a connection with a real object defined by its intrinsic qualities, rather than by the qualities we find there because we have, through projection, put them there. Indeed, one way of thinking about the goal of psychoanalysis is that it is to move the analyst to a significant degree outside the patient's fantasy world, so the analyst can be experienced as an object existing in its own right.

The individual's susceptibility to the power of words can be considered a measure of the difficulty he or she has in relating to other persons existing in their own right, rather than as characters in fantasy. Expressed another way, insistence that words have power and insistence that all encounters with other persons put us in a relationship with them are two aspects of one reality of the inner world, as is clearly exemplified in Johnson's insistence that words have power and her evident incorporation of strangers into her fantasy life.

Because the power of words is the power to trigger memories acting as or shaped into fantasy, the suffering embedded in fantasy is not dismissed by the absence of the words, although the identification of its source may change. The relationship indicates the source of the suffering, which is here transferred from the relationship as it exists in the remembered past to the source of the words spoken in the present. In this way, the original suffering and the remembered source of suffering are forgotten and reappear as the present source of the words. The vehicle for this is the reworking of memory into fantasy, which then triggers the response that seems to be caused by the words themselves.

In this context, speaking out may come to mean stopping others from speaking (Bowker & Levine, 2018). The hope is that by silencing their present-day voices, we can also silence the memory of a relationship transferred onto them. But, silencing a person in the present is not the same as silencing a memory. Silencing a memory means reducing or eliminating the intensity of the emotion attached to it. In other words, it is not the words spoken now that cause suffering. Rather, suffering expresses the continuing power of words spoken in the past, which is to say the internalization of the relationship the meaning of which is expressed in the words spoken then. The internal dialogue is the sound that must be silenced. Silencing the words in the mouths of those who would speak them in the present cannot do that.

Silence as Absence and Silence as Aggression

While silence may be a way of being present, it may also be experienced as absence. Silence experienced as absence is silence experienced as a danger to the self when the self's existence is dependent on the recognition or attention of another. Silence then becomes a fundamental and primitive sort of danger: the danger of not existing in a relationship needed to assure the feeling that we exist. Rather than the safety to be oneself experienced in an attentive relationship, there is the existential anxiety experienced in a relationship in which no ("audible" or manifest) attention is received. To cope with this anxiety and the danger that provokes it, it is necessary either to remain silent or to fill the silence with chatter in which little or no trace of the self is to be found.

What determines whether silence is experienced as presence or absence is (1) the quality of the communication that interrupts the silence, and (2) the capacity of the individual to be attentive to him- or herself, a capacity gained through the internalization of an attentive relationship. The weaker this latter capacity, the less tolerant of silence the individual can be, which is to say the more silence will be experienced as assault, most notably in the form of disparaging thoughts attributed to, or projected onto, the silent other.

In the analytic setting, what facilitates the movement from experiencing silence as absence to silence as presence is the way the analyst makes it clear, through interpretation, that silence indicates how she has been occupied not with herself but with the patient, or only with herself in so far as what is going on internally to her expresses the presence of the patient; in other words, through interpretation of the transference. This indicates that, the more complete the attention paid to the other person, the less the presence of the analyst, and the greater the presence of the patient. The more accurate the interpretation, the better it expresses the attention paid to the patient, and the more it affirms the patient's existence and presence. And the more accurate the interpretation, the more it provides evidence that attention is attuned to what is real and true in the patient, the more the hidden meaning of the patient's talk has been revealed and acknowledged.

But, the patient's talk is not only an invitation to having attention paid to what is real and true about his or her self; it is as often or more often an attempt to draw attention away from what is real and true. So, there is a complex communication that both seeks and avoids presence, that calls attention to a false self so the true self can remain hidden (Winnicott, 1965). This complexity in communication appears, for example, in the way we are never certain what it is that Danielle Johnson thought she should have said: We are never sure what it is she felt it was important to make known about her reaction to what she overheard. We are never told the words she failed to speak.

What does the term "accuracy" mean in the context of interpretations whose intent is to reveal what is real and true about the personality? It is possible, in response to this question, to argue that the term accuracy, in the usual sense, does not apply, but that what we need, instead, is an understanding of the construction of a special or new reality within a new relationship (Spence, 1982). Doing so may, however, miss something important in what accuracy refers to in the context of the analysis of the content of fantasy and enactment. What is most important about analytic interpretation is its effectiveness in transforming enactment into memory and thereby shifting the target of the patient's emotional investment from the present-day stand-in to the original object internalized as memory and fantasy.

Since both the stand-in and the original object are already "known," we need not attempt to assess interpretations against something outside memory or debate whether the process is capable of arriving at something accurate or true. The obstacle to accuracy of interpretation resides not in its subjectivity but in the different ways we know the present-day cause of our suffering and our memory of its source. Interpretation does not create new knowledge but provides access to something *already known*. It uncovers what we have hidden from ourselves. In an important sense, then, we "know" when an interpretation is accurate because the interpretation enables us to gain access to already existing knowledge, the "unthought known" (Bollas, 1987).

This act of interpreting is essentially an act of *integration,* the integration of memory, fantasy, and relating. To achieve this integration, interpretation connects what we do with what we think, thereby exposing the meaning embedded in doing and relating. Interpretation identifies or reveals the meaning embedded in experiences, memories, and fantasies. In doing so, interpretation reveals the nature of the forces operating at different levels and in different arenas of self-experience. It reveals how the whole is greater than the sum of the parts, and it thereby reveals what is real in the personality taken as a whole, what makes it what it is and allows us to know that we exist and are present.

If silence is a way of expressing absence (from relating), to speak is to be present, and in that sense to exist. As Johnson experienced the encounter after it occurred, what was intolerable was her absence from the relationship enacted in the grandfather's verbal assault on the boy. So, her failure to speak might be considered her reenactment of a failure to exist, and a recurrent fantasy formed out of her memory of her nonexistence in a relationship.

But, as we have tried to suggest, existence or nonexistence in a relationship means that we are either attended to or we are not. Who exists in a relationship depends on who receives attention and who does not. The goal, then, becomes making ourselves a center of attention, which is what Johnson did in her fantasy. In her fantasy, she experienced silence as aggression because silence implied that she did not exist in a relationship between the grandfather and grandson. And she experienced speaking out—or her missed opportunity to speak out and her subsequent fantasy of having spoken out—as the way to come to exist in that relationship. So, in fantasy, she came into existence by breaking her silence and imposing herself on a relationship from which she had been excluded.

Silencing Our Inner Voices

Thus far, we have considered speaking out as a defense against passivity. What we have not considered is that if we are to speak out, we must say something. And it matters what we say when we speak out. This raises again the question posed above: What is it that Johnson thinks she should have said? Johnson does not tell us what she should have said, perhaps because she considers it obvious. But it may not be. We can see the difficulty more clearly if we consider the one thing we know about what she should have said: words that would silence the grandfather. But, of course, her words would likely have failed to have that effect. Indeed, speaking to someone may be an invitation for them to continue talking. Given this dilemma, it is unsurprising that Johnson does not tell us what she should have said.

We can use language in ways that do not involve speaking to others. Most notably, we can speak *at* them in a way that conveys the message that no response other than silence will be tolerated. Perhaps this is the kind of speech that Johnson had in mind. The obvious alternative to the use of language to silence others is physical assault. We should not exclude the presence of such an assault in Johnson's fantasy about her encounter, but, lacking any report from her about the specific content of that fantasy, we cannot assume that physical assault is featured in it. And, in any case, physical assault takes us outside the bounds of speaking out as a response to witnessing unacceptable behavior. Having ruled out physical assault as a method to achieve the end of silencing those whose words are damaging, what remains is for us to find the words that, rather than inviting further speech from the target of our verbal aggression, will cause that target to remain silent. What are these words?

The first observation we might offer is that, if we insist on using language to block the use of language, then we must find words that have a special power. This special power may reside in us: We can use words in a way that silences others. Or, the power may reside in the use of special words, words for which, once spoken, there can be no response. We can put this another way. Perhaps Johnson is expressing a wish, the wish that she had the magic words and the magical power to use words to silence others. And, since, as we have suggested, the fantasy in which she uses words to silence external objects is the expression of a wish that she had the power over words that would allow her to silence her inner voices, especially those who shame her for passivity in the face of aggression, the wish is that she had a response to her inner voices that would silence them. As it turns out, it is no easier to silence inner voices than it is to silence the voices of others in the world outside. Indeed, it is much more difficult.

This raises the possibility that Johnson failed to speak out because she did not know what to say, that she did not have the power or know the special words that would silence the voices, whether external or internal. And her frustration was not primarily about the encounter she reports to her readers, but about an internal situation, where she does not know what to say or how to speak words to herself that would silence the inner voices whose speech blocks access to her center of initiative and action, thereby rendering her passive in the face of the aggression of others.

CHAPTER SEVEN

Abandonment

As we suggested in the last chapter, Danielle Johnson's insistence on the necessity of speaking out is but one expression of the emotional power of a broader moral imperative. This imperative is rooted in the conviction that the ability of authoritarian leaders, especially those connected to hate groups, to take power depends on the failure of those in whose presence they come to power to speak out against them. Perhaps the iconic expression of this moral imperative—one referenced frequently by those who insist on the importance of speaking out—was offered by Martin Niemöller in his famous poetic description of the Nazi path to power in Germany (*Holocaust Encyclopedia*, n.d.):

> *First they came for the Socialists, and I did not speak out—*
>
> *Because I was not a Socialist.*
>
> *Then they came for the Trade Unionists, and I did not speak out—*
>
> *Because I was not a Trade Unionist.*
>
> *Then they came for the Jews, and I did not speak out—*
>
> *Because I was not a Jew.*
>
> *Then they came for me—and there was no one left to speak for me.*

Central to Niemöller's account of the Nazi takeover is bystander guilt. Bystander guilt involves taking responsibility not for something we caused to happen, but for something we did not prevent from happening. One possible explanation for Niemöller's taking responsibility for the Nazis (his guilt for or complicity in what they did to their chosen victims) is his own anti-Semitism (*Holocaust Encyclopedia*, n.d.), which made it difficult for him to separate the reality of the Nazis from the hate that dominated his thoughts about their chosen victims. Then, the responsibility he bears for his fantasized attacks on Jews fosters his guilt for the real attacks on them by the Nazis. And, because of the consonance of his fantasy of assault with the reality of assault, he found the oppression of the Jews gratifying, and, as a result, he felt complicit and guilty. In other words, the Nazis enacted his fantasy while he not only stood by, but also took pleasure in their doing so. Even so, it does not follow that Niemöller was responsible for the violent attack on the Jews; nor does it follow that he could have prevented it.

The connection just suggested indicates that the bystander is not one who does nothing. The bystander, rather, may well be doing something: observing. Bystanders are not only those who do nothing when others are put at risk, they may also be those who watch others suffer. In Niemöller's case, bystanders watched while others were taken from their homes and separated from everything of value to them: their family, their property, their dignity, their humanity, and eventually their lives. This suggests that an element of voyeurism cannot in all cases be excluded from the relationship between bystanders and victims. It also suggests a possible distinction between bystanders and those who are simply uninvolved or disengaged, a distinction often disregarded by those concerned with bystander guilt.

To consider a distinction between the unaffected or the disengaged, on one hand, and the bystander, on the other, would be to challenge the presumption that everyone is "always already" engaged in active relationships with everyone else, that there is no possibility of being removed from others, particularly from victims and from those put at risk. Or, to be more precise: The only way to be removed from active engagement with others is to disengage in an act of willful blindness, a "looking" but not "seeing," or not being willing to see.

Were we to generalize from the Niemöller example—and it is of course hazardous to do so—we might say that bystander guilt and the moral imperative to speak out both have their emotional roots not in real-world responsibility for victimization, but in an unconscious fantasy of victimizing others and the pleasure taken in that fantasy. The more our guilt is rooted in the conflation of fantasy with reality, the more we confuse the omnipotence we have in fantasy with omnipotence we imagine ourselves to have in reality. The result of this confusion is the insistence that we are responsible for the reality of hatred, violence, and destruction over which we exert little or no influence.

The more we use hate groups, such as Nazis or neo-Nazis, as containers for our disavowed hate, the more intense our need to silence them and the more powerful our conviction that it is imperative that we speak out, since speaking out is the act by which we disavow our connection to them. We must silence them because we fear their words will activate our hate. And we know that failing to silence them empowers their hate because of the power of their words to activate hate in others. To silence them, we must speak out.

Bringing Back the Lost Object

Because speaking out is the method we use to disassociate from our hateful selves, failure to speak out puts us at risk of identification with those hateful selves. If, because of this identification, we become hateful, then we will, indeed, find ourselves in the situation in which Niemöller found himself, the situation of having "no one left to speak for me." This suggests how central is the lament expressed in the state of having no one who will speak for us, and how the insistence that we speak out is an expression of our anxiety about being without anyone to speak for us, anyone to protect us from our own internal objects and their manifestations in the external world.

Underlying the manifest content of the fantasy (bystander guilt), then, there is a less evident, but no less powerful, theme, which is the theme of abandonment. In the first parts of the poem, it is the bystander, represented by Niemöller himself, who abandons those who will be taken by the Nazis and in this respect abandoned to them. Then, at the end of the poem, it is Niemöller who finds himself alone and vulnerable in a world filled with hate and destruction. All of those who might have spoken out for him are gone.

Taking on the responsibility for speaking for others can be a way of expressing our wish that someone would take responsibility for us, as is clearly suggested in the poem. If this is the case, then the underlying driver for the insistence that people speak out is the absence in our lives of an advocate, someone we can rely on to speak out for us. Then, the matter turns out to be an expression not of guilt, but of a deeply embedded abandonment fantasy originating in an early experience of the absence of a dependable parental object. The poem provides a forceful account of an underlying anxiety about being alone in the face of destructive forces, which is the state of being without any reliable object to assure our safety in a world (both internal and external) with which we are ill-equipped to cope.

Thought about in this way, the poem describes taking responsibility for abandonment (guilt) as a defense against anxiety that we will be abandoned. And, the appropriation of the poem by individuals and groups preoccupied with preventing the triumph of destructive forces in society indicates how intolerable it is to acknowledge that the loss of a protective relationship was not our doing but the result of the operation of forces beyond our control, and that, therefore, there is nothing we can do about it. Yet, only by accepting that there was nothing we could have done about it can we relieve ourselves of culpability and disengage from the self we hold culpable.

Indeed, the emotional need to reject the idea that we can do nothing to prevent a catastrophe that has already occurred (abandonment and loss) drives the insistence on bystander guilt in the face of catastrophes that are taking place in the present or that threaten to occur in the future. Guilt operates here as a defense against passivity; but, if it is intense enough, it can block contact with the self, which is our internal source of the active orientation in the world.

Bystander guilt, then, is emotionally equivalent to the insistence that there is always something we can do. This something we can do is to bring back the lost object, and in so doing reestablish our own lost state of grace. We bring back the object by becoming that object and speaking out for others in the way the object was meant to speak out for us. If assuring ourselves that there is always something we can do becomes too important, then reality-testing must be sacrificed. What we do will be disconnected from the possibilities for meaningful action (or inaction) embedded in reality, which also means that what we do will be unlikely to bring about the hoped-for result. This is not surprising, since what we do is to stand in for a lost object, an action unlikely to cause it to return.

Annihilation Anxiety and Hate

We have suggested that the link of bystander guilt to abandonment fantasy indicates a connection to the issues surrounding passivity considered in the previous chapter. As we point out there, an important component of what is typically referred to as bystander guilt is shame for identification with our passive selves. So far as the shame we feel is a primary emotional driver, it is not surprising that the issue of whether, in reality, our intervention would have altered the course of events seems of little importance. When shame is the driver, the damage we fail to prevent is damage we inflict on ourselves. Shame for our passivity has little to do with the likelihood that our action would alter the outcome of what we observe in reality, and much to do with the identification of ourselves with the passivity of the victim, an identification that could have been disrupted by speaking or acting, even if speaking or acting would have had no effect on the outcome for the victim.

When we take shame more fully into account, the link of bystander guilt to the loss of a powerful figure on whom we can depend to speak out for us moves to the forefront. Whatever the form this abandonment may have taken (actual physical absence or forms of emotional unresponsiveness), when it is significant enough and early enough, it can provoke an intense kind of anxiety, which is the anxiety about psychic existence and the possibility of emotional destruction sometimes referred to as annihilation anxiety. Annihilation anxiety moves the experience of loss and destruction from the past to the future, in part to make prevention of the catastrophe possible (Winnicott, 1974). The more powerful the fear of emotional destruction, the more powerful the identification, whether positive or negative, with the victim. In the case of positive identification, passivity dominates in our response to threatening situations as do feelings of shame for our passivity. In the case of negative identification (reaction formation), aggression dominates.

Annihilation anxiety can provoke intensely destructive impulses directed at the parental object who has abdicated his or her responsibilities and is therefore accountable for the state of bottomless dread in which the child finds him- or herself. At the same time, annihilation anxiety can be a response to those destructive impulses the presence of which is experienced as the cause of the loss of the good object. When intense states of aggression against the object on which we depend for our emotional and physical well-being coalesce into characters in a fantasy drama of loss and destruction, those fantasy characters can appear, through projection, as figures in the outside world.

But the more we use hate groups and those who represent them to contain our own hate by speaking out against them, the more we *need* hate groups to express their hate toward their victims, who are also surrogates for our own victim selves. This suggests another, related, reason speaking out becomes an imperative. It is through speaking out that we engage with and, in this way, empower the containers for our hate, provoke them to enact and, sometimes, escalate their expressions of hate, thereby validating our use of them to externalize our own hate.

This dynamic was evident in the predominance of disavowal in the rhetoric following the violence in Charlottesville, Virginia in 2017, which began as a confrontation between neo-Nazis and the KKK, on one side, and those opposed to them on the other. That rhetoric featured the demand that all those who are not members of hate groups aggressively disavow their connection with those groups, that they announce that those groups, and *only* those groups, are responsible for all the hate, and that they declare that such expressions of hate, if not the very existence of hate groups, will not be tolerated. In some cases—most notably, in the advocacy and support for the anti-fascist group known as Antifa—it was held that the mere presence of hate groups may (or must) be opposed with violence.

Our point is not that there is no place for opposition to hate groups, nor that we should not be concerned with their potential for violence, which is all too real. Nor is our point that the violence in Charlottesville was somehow equally the responsibility of the hate groups and those who demonstrated against them. That we use hate groups to contain our disavowed hate does not call into question the reality of the threat of violence they pose, nor does it imply that those opposing them constitute an equal threat, or any threat at all. Rather, our point is that, when opposition to hate groups is driven by unconscious identification with them, the actions we take to express our concern will likely have the effect of drawing attention to these groups, provoking them to express their hate through violence, and enabling some of those in opposition to them to justify their own violent acts.

Put simply, when motivated by identification, the unconscious end of our engagement with hate groups is to provoke them to act out their hate. The cycle of hate this sets in motion raises the stakes and intensifies conflict, when our purpose should be to meet the provocation offered by hate groups with the exercise of our capacity to contain our hate, so that the fuel it would otherwise provide to those groups is not made available to them. What determines the effectiveness of our response to hate is not whether we speak out or remain silent, but whether we exercise the capacity to contain our hate, rather than act it out and play along with the contentious drama enacted by hate groups. When we contain our hate, what we do—whether that is to remain silent or to speak out—is not an acting out of our hate, but an expression of thoughts and emotions not rooted in hate.

When Donald Trump responded to the violence in Charlottesville by claiming a false equivalence between the hate groups and those demonstrating against them, it was reasonable to see in this his support for those hate groups and, therefore, his identification with them. Indeed, there exists a considerable body of evidence that hate is a primary driver of many, if not most, of Trump's statements and actions, and that these statements and actions were driven by destructive intent and would lead to significant harm. There is also reason to believe that a primary goal of Trump's statements and actions is to provoke hate in others, to make them hate him because he, in a sense, thrives on being hated.

When Trump not only failed to disavow the hate groups, but instead aligned himself with them, he did so by failing to say the words that would clearly disassociate him from them. In response to this failure, many insisted that he speak those words, and made it a point to tell him what those words were. According to Arnold Schwarzenegger, Trump should have said: "As President of the United States, and as a Republican, I reject the support of white supremacists. The country that defeated Hitler's armies is no place for Nazi flags. The party of Lincoln won't stand with those who carry the battle flags of the failed Confederacy" (Gibson, 2017). According to *The Washington Post* (2017), Trump should have said: "To wink at racism or to condone it through silence, or false moral equivalence, or elision, as some do, is no better and no more acceptable than racism itself. Just as we can justly identify radical Islamic terrorism when we see it, and call it out, so can we all see the racists in Charlottesville, and understand that they are anathema in our society, which depends so centrally on mutual respect."

These are only two of numerous pronouncements of what was the right thing to say and the related insistence that Trump should say the right thing, even if he neither meant it nor understood it, and that his saying the right thing would somehow make a difference. While there is good reason to expect a president to disassociate himself from hate groups and to publicly condemn them, the persistent drumbeat of citizens, celebrities, and public figures telling him what he should have said, by indicating what they would have said, also suggests how powerful was the urge to use Trump as a vehicle for distancing ourselves from our own hate.

It is worth noting that what Trump was told he should have said were words that would insist on the goodness of the nation: "We are the nation of Lincoln, the nation that defeated slavery." "We are the nation that defeated the Nazis." "Racists are anathema to our society." In other words, he should have offered a fantasy of a nation that is a beacon of goodness, a fantasy to set against the Nazi fantasy of racial purification, hatred, and division. Trump had difficulty doing so because he had difficulty seeing the good; and, he had difficulty seeing the good because of the intensity of his emotional involvement with dark fantasy (Levine, 2018). In the dark fantasy, the world is a dangerous place; those responsible for our safety and well-being are incompetent and corrupt. They are little interested in us and wholly preoccupied with themselves. In the world of the dark fantasy there is no good, there is only bad and the struggle among those who are bad over the surrogate forms of gratification available where there is nothing good to nourish the self, surrogates typically bound up with destructive forms of greed, with envy, and with hate.

Because it is an emotional response to abandonment, there is a sense in which the core of annihilation anxiety is a special kind of loneliness. This is the loneliness of those who find themselves in an unresponsive world. It is the loneliness of absence, of being bereft of a connection that keeps us spiritually alive, of the loss of a world once made safe by the presence in it of someone who would stand up, speak out, and care for us.

As we suggest in Chapter Two, the result of the loss of a life-sustaining relationship is the loss of the sense that we are attended to—seen, heard, and known—in a way that acknowledges our presence. Not being attended to is the *active* denial of our existence. When others do not attend to us in this active sense of the word, our vital spirit or self is diminished. When the self is diminished or even lost, there can be nothing about us that indicates our presence in our world. We are, instead, faceless and nameless creatures neither known by nor knowable to self or other.

Projection of this experience of nonexistence onto others populates the world with faceless and nameless creatures whose intent is to impose on us an endless reenactment of the experience of loss of self in the eyes of others. These creatures are the ones designated by the pronoun "they" in Niemöller's account of the Nazi takeover. Not only do "they" take over our world, but in their act of taking over, they make us one of them. All distinctions of identity are eliminated, and all become the same, designated by an impersonal plural pronoun.

We suggest above that the energy driving bystander guilt has its source in the anxiety that there is nothing we can do to prevent a catastrophe that has already occurred. To defend ourselves against recognition that this catastrophe is not preventable because it already occurred, we seek refuge in a life organized to prevent the catastrophe from occurring by making the fantasy that it has not yet occurred, and so can be prevented, into a reality. To do so, we must transform the feeling of bottomless loss associated with not existing into the activity of finding and/or creating a new world in which the loss will not occur.

The vehicle for this activity is the regressed group. The regressed group is the group of shared loss. This group not only defends its members against knowing what they have lost, it also promises to repair the damage done by offering group solidarity and belonging as a substitute for the lost connection. Recognition of group membership and shared possession of a valued group self mutes the residue of the loss of existence/presence in early relationships. Thus, the regressed group simultaneously offers to repair the damage done early in life and to recreate the damaging relationship subject to the fantasy that the problem contained in it is its own solution. In the regressed group, you will still feel bereft, but you will not be alone. By sharing that feeling, you will come to experience it as the opposite of what it is.

Abandonment and Regression in Contemporary Thought

As discussed in the Introduction, much contemporary political and moral thought, particularly thought that falls into what we may classify as the (overlapping) traditions of the absurd, the postmodern, and the post-structural (see Bowker, 2014, 2016; Lacan, 1988; Lyotard, 1984) begins with the assertion of a fundamental "lack" or experience of abandonment and continues by chastising those who would deny it, while valorizing the recognition of this shared absence.

If what is absurd about life is that "the human cry" (*l'appel humain*) is met with "the unreasonable silence of the world" (Camus, 1955, p. 28), or if our "nostalgia for unity" clashes with the absence of a loving object, leaving us in a "fragmented universe" where only "the contradiction" between our needs and what is missing "binds [us] together" (p. 50), it is hard not to hear in such words a lament about the loss of the environment afforded by primary love, the loss of an object to secure that environment, in other words the loss of a home. Now, our worlds are dominated by destructive emotions and dark fantasies, and we are bound to the world that has abandoned us "as only hatred can weld two creatures together" (p. 21).

Hate is the tie that binds the abandoned to the abandoner. If so, hate is the predominant emotion connecting the abandoned self to the part of the self that still wishes for the abandoner to return, a wish, of course, that also represents a betrayal of the abandoned self, which would reject and never forgive this object. Since the target for our hate is absent, and since two parts of ourselves are at war with each other, this hate remains inside. If hate is what "binds" the abandoned self to the abandoning self, self-relating will of necessity include a substantial measure of self-hatred, which means that the self will identify both with a hating, ashamed, abandoned self and with a hateful, guilty, abandoning self.

In response to this tortured psychic condition, Camus recommends living "*sans appel*" (without appeal, call, or cry). While the French term "*appel*," in this case, is reasonably translated as "appeal," it is illuminating to consider what it might mean were we to understand it as "call" or "cry." The infant or child who cries but whose cries are not attended to must learn to cease crying out for attention. But, if the infant must cease crying for an abandoning object, his tremendous rage directed at the object that abandoned him in his state of distress becomes the center of his psychic life, which is spent "rebelling" against abandoning objects by publicly "calling them out" or "speaking out" against them wherever he may find them.

The absurd, postmodern, and post-structuralist repudiations of God, Reason, the "Subject," and other putative illusions also involve an effort to deprive others. Envy that those who are either privileged enough or naïve enough not to consider themselves so abandoned must be disabused of their illusions, which are construed to be dangerous precisely because the destructive envy that drives the impulse to strip them of their beloved objects is projected on the victims, who are held responsible for the loss of our own.

Camus, like many contemporary moral and political thinkers, makes the act of speaking out against experiences or instances of abandonment the center of what it means to be alive. What it means to be alive, then, is to find and subsume oneself into a regressed group, which is the group of shared loss. This group is the substitute for the lost home and the abandoning object. The group will not abandon us, so long as we adhere to its fundamental assumptions and carry out its purpose, which is to share its experience of loss and abandonment with others, to bring others into the group.

As we have alluded to earlier, for Judith Butler, in the face of loss and destruction, "my own foreignness to myself is, paradoxically, the source of my ethical connection with others" (2004, p. 46). A shared identification with suffering, which is not merely an identification with others but with their suffering and victimized selves, is valued here because it forces us to lose ourselves into the regressed group. Here, the loss of self and of the capacity to relate means that we may form a regressed group of collectively "undone" people whose shared "loss has made a tenuous 'we' of us all" (p. 20). Something of this notion is summarized in Camus' grandiose slant on the Cartesian *cogito*: "I rebel [against absence and absurdity], therefore we exist" ("*Je me révolte, donc nous sommes*") (1956, p. 22).

Camus, like others, is ambivalently attracted to the idea of exile and homelessness, recommending that we internalize the rejection experienced by an object that did not attend to us or provide us with a home good enough for us to begin to develop an autonomous self. Instead, we travel to the frontiers and "distant regions" (1955, p. 10), live on the margins, take shelter in faraway places where there is little or no chance of having a life of our own or bringing ourselves to bear on the world. These "deserts" and "deadly" climates of the mind (pp. 22, 29) derive their barrenness from the fact that they are, like those who inhabit them, more dead than alive.

CHAPTER EIGHT

Survivors

Guilt associated with failing to prevent a catastrophe bears a somewhat complicated relationship to guilt associated with surviving a catastrophe when others failed to do so (survivor guilt). The violent forces responsible for loss of life were also present for the survivors, who, just as easily, might have been their targets or succumbed to them. Bystanders may also have survived destructive forces, but they may not have been their targets and might not have been at risk. Formulating the matter in this way places it on the plane of the external reality of cause and effect. On another level, a bystander who was not, in fact, at risk may nonetheless feel that he or she was. If there exists a strong enough identification between bystander and victim, the distinction between bystander and survivor may not be as strong psychologically as it is in the external reality of cause and effect, intent and consequence.

In *The Minimal Self*, Christopher Lasch understands the contemporary "survival mentality," which is a pervasive "rhetoric of crisis and survival," as an encouragement to experience life as a state of siege, an unending "succession of crises" (1984, p. 64). Lasch interprets survival discourses both as memorials to the horrors of the concentration camp, which still looms large in our historical memory, and as expressions of anxiety about the fact that social, economic, and political spheres of life are increasingly dominated by large and powerful organizations. In fact, Lasch argues, the rhetoric of survival and victimization served as "a survival strategy in its own right" (p. 62), since a "survival ethic" may simplify complex interpersonal and political dilemmas, since survivors are permitted, if not encouraged, to believe that the primary—and perhaps only—goal is to survive.

Perhaps surprisingly, Lasch contends that "the siege mentality is much stronger in those who know Auschwitz [or any concentration camp] only at second hand [i.e. as witnesses or bystanders] than in those who lived through it. It is the survivors who see their experience as a struggle not to survive but to stay human … It is the survivors who try to 'give meaning to survival,' while those who come after them and live under conditions seemingly more secure see meaning only in survival itself" (1984, p. 128). The ideals, attachments, and achievements needed to integrate life-threatening experiences into a meaningful life, according to Lasch, elude not those who have suffered the most incredible torments, but those who identify with such survivors across some distance, and, sometimes, while facing less desperate circumstances (see also Bowker, 2014, pp. 95–96).

Such accounts stand in complex relation to more thorough studies of survivors of the Holocaust, such as those conducted by C. Fred Alford. Alford notes, from studying hundreds of archived interviews with survivors, that many experienced themselves, for instance, as having "died at Auschwitz" (2009, p. 58). The question that seems to present itself to survivors, then, is not simply one of how to go on living or how to contend with survivor guilt but why: It is the question of "whether the pain of living has been worth the price" (p. 59). Where Lasch's and Alford's accounts do coincide, however, is in their assessments of many Holocaust survivors as persons who seek more than mere survival, who struggle to live in a robust sense even amid unwelcome visitations of past trauma and terror, and who often undertake complex psychological strategies to permit themselves—or at least a part of their selves—to "have a life."

Separation and Mourning

The theme of separation and loss has been emphasized by those engaged with the issue of survivor guilt. Thus, Alfred Garwood suggests that survivor guilt persists "primarily because survivors are unable to grieve and mourn their losses successfully" (1996, p. 246). William Niederland offers a parallel conclusion about survivors when he states that, in the great majority of cases, "it is the survival itself that stands at the core of the inner conflict."

Survivors—both writers are concerned with survivors of the Holocaust—identify themselves with the "beloved dead," whom they feel they should join in death. This is so much the case that Niederland found in those of his patients who were survivors the "phenomenal attitude" of "walking corpses," specifically: "taciturn behavior, pale complexion, shuffling gate." His observations led him to conclude that survival "is consciously felt as a betrayal of dead parents and siblings" (1981, p. 421).

Identification with the dead is an important aspect of the emotional residue of the catastrophe for those who survive. It can also attract those who were not at risk into an involvement with survivors. Those drawn to such an involvement can use the catastrophe of life-destroying events in the world outside to manage their own personal catastrophes, which they survived—or, at least, they wish or believe they did—while others did not—or at least they wish or believe they did not. This possibility suggests a complexity in the construction of the "survivor," since the survivor may have survived physically, but may not have survived emotionally. Indeed, those survivors Niederland describes as taking on the qualities of the dead may be expressing not only an identification with and a feeling of having betrayed the dead, but also the fact that they did not survive, if we take psychic existence as our measure. Then, what we refer to as survivor guilt is not really guilt at all, but a state of mind of those who continue to exist physically, although they have not truly survived. In Samuel Juni's words: "What we have here are survivors who act out a script of guilt rather than survivors who actually experience guilt" (2016, p. 328).

The different aspects of the survivor experience all involve the failure to mourn loss, which may be linked to a too-intense identification with the dead and their suffering that blocks any possibility that the survivor will be able to bring him- or herself back to life in the aftermath of loss: "Whenever losses are remembered, the overwhelming feelings of powerlessness and annihilation fears that were experienced at the time of the events together with the highly effective defence of self-blame are mobilized" (Garwood, 1996, p. 246). The dangers associated with coming to terms with loss, especially dangers associated with the kind of remembering involved in mourning loss, impedes separation from the lost object and fosters an intensified identification with it (Freud, 1917e). Then, survivor guilt refers to the emotional consequences of the attempt to create distance from whatever impulses are active in the survivor to go on with his or her life—indeed, to have a life—when doing so definitively separates the survivor from those who did not survive. Separating themselves from the dead means accepting that the dead are dead, which is experienced psychologically as causing their death. And, in one sense, this equation is correct: Mourning the dead *makes* them dead to the survivors and creates a definitive psychic boundary between those who did and those who did not survive.

To summarize the notion of survivor guilt: Survivor guilt involves taking responsibility for the deaths of those who did not survive, responsibility that the individual feels not because he or she actually caused the deaths of those who failed to survive, but because the survivor did survive, regardless of whether his or her survival was a matter of his or her own doing. This taking responsibility expresses itself in the effort to bring the dead back to life, or to keep them alive when they are not, by identifying with them.

All of this makes sense if we understand the death of the body to represent the death of the psyche or spirit. Even in accepting the death of the body, there can be resistance to acknowledging death of the spirit, which is kept alive in the mind of the survivor so long as the dead remain alive there. The real sense of responsibility is for the death of the spirit; indeed, much of what has been written about the rejection or refusal to mourn as an ethical imperative clearly points us in this direction.

So, we need to understand the various aspects of survivor guilt as aspects of the individual's connection to his or her self or vital spirit and to the events that led to the severing of that connection. It is the impulse to go on living, the life force within the survivor, that must be countered if the spirit of the dead is to remain alive in the psyche of the living. The effort to counter the impulse to go on living, because it constitutes a betrayal of the dead, can take different forms (Juni, 2016), of which we will consider three:

1. The effort to counter the impulse to go on living may rely on the conviction that the mere fact of having survived meant that others did not, so that whatever benefits the survivor has had in his or her life are the result of the deprivation of others. Here, a conflictual element is assumed to be embedded in the desire for the good things, which are conceived in such a way that they are in limited supply and that their acquisition is a zero-sum game. If their acquisition is a zero-sum game, then merely having them indicates responsibility for those who do not, an idea that underlies the notion of privilege sometimes used to impose guilt on members of groups who have not been dispossessed by past oppression (a matter taken up more thoroughly in the next chapter).

This quality of the good things—that having them equals dispossessing others of them—suggests a connection to the most primitive good thing, which is love and attention as expressed through the provision of primitive nurturing and the possession of the good object implied by it. The implied inconsistency between the nature of the good things and the idea of sharing them follows from the experience that the good things become available because we need them and, in this sense, that we have a kind of power over them. In Winnicott's formulation, this is the power to "create the world" (1986, p. 40), a power that can hardly be shared. When more mature emotional experience is shaped by this more primitive experience, it must be true that one person's acquisition of the good things causes others to lose them and that our power to create the good things for ourselves is our power to deprive others of them.

2. The effort to counter the impulse to go on living may rest on an unconscious assumption that bad things happen to bad people, which implies that those who are victims must be bad (Lerner, 1980). This assumption may be linked to the one just briefly considered since, in primitive emotional life, nothing in the realm of gratification and deprivation is experienced to happen by chance. Instead, all experiences of good and bad are taken to be intended. In the primitive world, we get good things because we are good (deserving), and getting good things means we are good. By contrast, we are deprived of good things because we are bad (undeserving) so that being deprived of good things means we are bad. No more evidence is needed in support of the link of deprivation to the badness of the deprived than deprivation itself.

A construction along these lines is clearly the motivating factor in the effort to substitute the term "survivor" for the term "victim," for example in accounts of those who have experienced sexual assault. The hope is that in changing the word used we can also change the nature of the experience, at least as that is instantiated in memory and fantasy, by purging it of what is arguably its most emotionally salient quality—passivity—thereby purging it of the shame associated with passivity. Use of the term "survivor" in this context implies the possibility of not surviving, since, otherwise, the accomplishment of surviving would not mean much. Some survive the experience, while others do not. There can be no pride in survival, however, where there is no shame in failure to survive. In this construction we also shift the focus of survival from our physical to our emotional existence, since the problem for survivors of sexual assault is not the problem of remaining physically alive but of remaining emotionally alive.

3. The effort to counter the impulse to go on living may arise from fantasies, however unconscious, of omnipotence that, as in the case of bystander guilt, always make the individual responsible for harm done to others. That is, it is assumed that the individual could always have prevented it. Fantasies of omnipotence counter the shame associated with victimization shared by those who survive when they are strongly identified with those who did not. The role of omnipotence is linked by Garwood (1996, p. 246) to annihilation anxiety. Thus "*survivor self-blame*" had the initial primary and principal function of reducing the pain and anguish of intolerable powerlessness in the face of annihilation risk and overwhelming loss. Garwood links survivor self-blame to the same primitive emotional experiences just summarized when he notes how "powerlessness in later life evokes unconscious memories of [the] earliest vulnerable state and primal agony, accompanied by overwhelming emotions, mobilizing powerful defences, often self-blame and consequential guilt" (p. 249). He suggests that the "central traumatizing experiences were powerlessness in the face of annihilation risk, reinforced by object loss, [which] would lead one to predict that the defences generated would be primarily omnipotent phantasies as a response to powerlessness, encapsulation as a response to annihilation threat and anxiety and attempted reparation of losses. The psychic self-empowerment necessary for self-blame is achieved through omnipotent phantasy" (p. 249). Unconscious omnipotent fantasy, then, is connected to guilt as the individual's responsibility expands with the expansion of the individual's power to shape reality.

Survivor Groups

The struggle between the impulse to go on living and the impulse to do what must be done to join the dead plays a significant role in political conflict when the political setting becomes the site on which those who have survived enact their identification with those who have not. This drama plays itself out along two dimensions. Along the first, the individual who escaped a community dominated by the experience of psychic or spirit death sees it as his or her mission to serve that community and to uphold its constituting fantasy that the emotional damage suffered by those remaining there is not damage at all but the source of the community's strength. Along the second, survivor guilt experienced by those who have escaped the community of shared loss is projected onto those who are not and have never been a part of that community, who then become responsible for the damage done to it.

This projection of guilt creates a particularly strong link between survivors and those who are designated to contain their guilt. This link takes the form of a preoccupation with, and devotion of life to, the attachment of guilt to the outsiders designated to contain it, an attachment that tends to disconnect insistence on their guilt from any clearly defined and reality-based ends. The idea of survivor guilt can, then, help us understand the importance that the attribution of guilt plays in politics where assigning guilt often overwhelms the use of politics to achieve specific policy goals involving, for instance, the repair of damaged communities or the safeguarding of future generations against the fate suffered by those who did not survive.

The involvement of survivor guilt in politics engages the matter of the *survivor group*. Here, we use this term to refer not to the group of those who have survived, but more broadly to the group organized around a shared fantasy about the meaning of surviving and its central role in defining what it means to be alive. This is the fantasy that equates surviving—along with the struggle to survive and the enactment and reenactment of that struggle—with what it means to be alive. Outside of the survivor group, we use the word "survival" to refer to living, but in a minimal sense. We may have survived, but if we have only or merely survived, we have lost something vital. As suggested above, the survivor group is also a group of those who did not survive; they are alive and not alive. They are not alive because they are so intensely involved with death.

The survivor group is a group whose members are defined by a preponderance of survivor guilt in their emotional lives. More specifically, members of the survivor group evince a high degree of ambivalence about their connection to being emotionally alive. Paradoxically, the survivor is, in an important sense, someone who has not survived, or who cannot allow him- or herself to be alive where life means anything more than surviving. So, the survivor equates surviving with being alive. The survivor "gets by," but does not thrive emotionally.

Survivors may devote their lives to honoring those who did not survive, or to saving or rescuing those whose lives are similarly at risk. In other words, they may devote their lives to acting out the drama of saving themselves by saving others who act as stand-ins for themselves or containers for the precious life they no longer have. By doing so, they may find themselves honoring the lives of the dead, and also honoring their own deaths. All goals pursued must be consistent with keeping the dead alive through identification with them, which has the effect of preventing those who are physically alive (survivors) from the experience of being emotionally or psychically alive, or of having a life of their own.

Beyond its complex relationship to death and survival, the survivor group is organized around a specific experience of death and destruction: survivors of the Holocaust, survivors of slavery and racial oppression, survivors of genocide, of rape, of natural disaster. But simply because you did not die in a catastrophe does not make you a member of the survivor group. For that, a powerful identification with the dead (most notably in the form of survivor guilt) is required.

Part of what is at issue here is the centrality of victimizing, threatening, or traumatizing experiences in the psychic lives of survivors, and, indeed, in the lives of others. Thus, Elie Wiesel argued in his (1986) Nobel Peace Prize acceptance speech that "wherever men or women are persecuted because of their race, religion, or political views, that place must—at that moment—become the center of the universe" (quoted in Reilly, 2016). The call to make every site of persecution, oppression, or victimization a "center of the universe" expresses a fantasy that the experience of the survivor will become central to everyone in the world. Here, the (moral) "gravity" of victims' suffering "pulls" everyone into the survivor group, incorporating all into a single moral universe where everything "revolves" around survivors' experiences, beliefs, and fantasies.

On one hand, what exists at the center of the universe does not move, but remains stationary, while other objects revolve around it; on the other hand, to the extent that this center has mass, it gradually pulls in everything in its gravitational field. The difference we highlight here is the difference between being the center of the universe and being a "center of initiative" (Kohut, 1977, p. 99), which is the difference between surviving amid a survivor group and being an autonomous self, capable of initiating thought, action, and change in the world.

Placing the survival of victimization, persecution, or trauma at the center of a moral universe encourages persons and groups to become, in Cathy Caruth's words, centers or "site[s] of [shared] trauma" (1995, p. 11), rather than centers or sites of autonomous being, doing, and relating. What is more, while this fantasy of change offers a kind of hope, it is, in many respects, a deeply conservative fantasy, for its primary objective is to secure the identification with survivors and victims, rather than to act in ways that make meaningful differences for the self or others.

For thinkers like Caruth, the "truth" one gleans from surviving trauma is, itself, conceived to be of great value, and is what is shared with the survivor group. Ideally, following this line of thought, the truth of surviving trauma should be shared with everyone, although it is essentially impossible to articulate because survivors are no longer capable of thinking about, representing, or communicating their experiences. Instead, they carry "an impossible history within them, or they become themselves the symptom of a history that they cannot entirely possess" (Caruth, 1995, p. 5).

At a collective level, we are encouraged to understand ourselves as living in a "posttraumatic century" (Felman, 1995, p. 13), and, so, we must "understand history as the history of trauma" (Caruth, 1996, p. 60) and "history as holocaust" (Felman & Laub, 1992, p. 95), such that "history," itself, becomes "precisely the way we are implicated in each other's traumas" (p. 24). That is, according to the logic of the survivor group, the truth of the trauma or violence survived is what must be retained, memorialized, and transmitted if the survivors' survival is to mean anything. And what must be transmitted, according to Walter Benn Michaels, is "not the normalizing knowledge of the horror but the horror itself" (quoted in Leys 2000, p. 268). Since outsiders cannot—and, indeed, some argue that even survivors cannot—know their survival experience, we can only share with each other experiences of horror, breakdowns of language and reason, and the destruction of our selves. Thinking, relating, and expressions of self distort the survivor's truth, which is "a symptom which must not ... be cured but simply transmitted, passed on" (pp. 268–269). Thus, the moral demand that survivor groups undertake a deliberate "infection," "contaminat[ion]" (p. 268), and "contagion" (Caruth, 1995, p. 10; Terr, 1988) of others by transmitting traumatic material across persons and groups is underwritten by the hope (fantasy) that in doing so the experience of survival will become and remain central to the experience of life in the world, as it has come to be central to the inner lives of survivors.

If survivors have been through an experience of death, the residue of that experience cannot be separated from the loss of the feeling that we exist, which can be linked to a heightened need to find our existence in the attention paid to us by others. Recognition of our unique presence becomes the need to be the center of attention for all. The survivor group is the group of those who did not survive the loss of primary love, which instilled in us the conviction that our existence was of no consequence, that we do not matter. With this conviction comes an intensified need to matter in precisely the ways we did not. The key, then, is the impulse to seek attention for our loss and in this way to compensate for it while also reinforcing our attachment to it.

Survivor Politics

Some survivor groups take on a political purpose and some political movements translate the emotional configuration of the survivor group into a political agenda. There is, in other words, a special politics—*survivor politics*—suited to the emotional agenda of survivor groups. The purpose of survivor politics is to make the inner world of the survivors their external reality. The dominant reality of the inner world of the survivor is that it is unsafe to exist (be alive) there. It is the reality of the dark fantasy of an embattled life whose only safety lies in the individual's ability to hide awareness of existence and to prevent it from influencing doing and relating. This hiding of life takes the form of the repression of all signs of vitality. In suppressing all signs of vitality, the living become the dead.

Repression of vitality is an emotional response to a basic disruption in the connection to the good object. This is where fantasies of the omnipotence of justice can begin to play a role as a mechanism for fixing the inner world. Seeking "justice" can become an activity through which the individual can hope to retrieve what has been lost: contact with his or her inner vitality. Then, politics understood as the pursuit of justice becomes a setting in which it is possible to come to life.

The possibility that politics can be used in this way makes it a particularly suitable locus for survivor groups for whom the central struggle is between life and death. It is a reason survivor groups may come to see themselves as political groups or may emerge within the setting of political engagement. When this is the case, there develops a conviction that outside of political engagement, the individual may *have a life*, but it is only through political engagement that the individual truly *comes to life* (see e.g. Arendt, 1998).

Politics facilitates the putting into place of a manic defense against feelings associated with the loss of the relationship on which, early in life, our connection with our vital center depended. This makes politics literally a matter of life and death. And, of course, to the extent that justice-seeking agendas and activities are aimed not at ameliorating or correcting injustices in the real world but at reviving the justice-seekers' emotional vitality, their external forms will be misaligned with, or perhaps even contrary to, their stated aims. Marked by a sense of failure to achieve the unconsciously desired end, they may become repetitive, hyperbolic, provocative, aggressive, and destructive.

The fantasy of survivor politics is that justice can limit the burden of self-hate, thereby making it possible for the individual to reconnect with his or her vital center and retrieve the feeling of being alive that only this connection can secure. The result is a social defense against annihilation anxiety that invests the survivor group with its reason to be. When the marriage of politics with justice gives meaning to the group, it becomes important that everyone share the need for this defense. Hence, the insistence on the moral imperative of civic engagement, and the treatment of disengagement as a moral failure.

Where survivor guilt plays a large role, participation or engagement can take on a special meaning involving identification with the survivor group. This identification can lead to a markedly conservative stance at the center of what, on cursory examination, may seem a forward-looking or even progressive agenda. Where progress requires separation from a group organized around an experience of destruction, progress can take on the emotional significance of abandonment and betrayal. This abandonment and betrayal parallels the experience of the child who escapes the dysfunctional family but carries a significant measure of survivor guilt for having done so. In the larger societal context, abandoning the family is reexperienced in separation from the survivor group. If participation means remaining in the group, it demands a distinctly conservative orientation.

This problem becomes clear when we consider that the core idea of progressive political movements is justice, even though there can be no justice for those who have not survived. There are, of course, those who would insist on justice for the dead, by which they have in mind punishing those who are, or who are imagined to be, responsible for causing their death. But, of course, justice for the dead neither repairs damage nor retrieves anything important for them, a fact that only reinforces the conclusion that justice for the dead is, really, justice for those still living who are strongly identified with the dead. Those who are still living but are strongly identified with the dead, however, cannot be repaired or otherwise brought to life without losing their connection with the dead, which is essential to them. This means that justice for the dead does not suggest any forward movement, but rather reinforces a kind of stasis: that the dead remain dead and that we remain connected with them. It is in this sense—but not only this sense—that justice can represent a deeply conservative goal.

Justice for the dead means assuring that all those still living must identify with them. Only if that happens can the onus attached to their failure to survive be lifted. This onus is complex but, as we have suggested above, may be linked to unconscious beliefs that it was our survival that caused their death, that those who did not survive deserved their death, or that it was within our power to guarantee their survival. In seeking justice for the dead, then, there may reside a hope that such justice, once achieved, will free those who survived but remain identified with the dead to move on with their lives. This hope is the hope that, if we could go back in time and undo the damage that caused death to those who did not survive, we could liberate those whose attachment to them is based on survivor guilt. Put another way, if we can disconnect the problematic judgment attached to those who did not survive, we can disconnect that same judgment attached to those identified with them. This means that, psychologically, bringing the dead to life is the only way we can bring those who have taken on responsibility for their death back to life. In this sense, the "survival syndrome" as Niederland (1981) terms it, blocks mourning because to mourn the dead is to accept their death and to accept death is to preclude any repair of the dead that would free the living from their death.

All of this suggests the organization of internal experience around a social defense centered on the fantasy of the *omnipotence of justice*. The fantasy of the omnipotence of justice is linked to the hope that what is wrong can be fixed if the institutions of justice force others to carry the burden of the bad or defective self. Where this conviction holds, the solution embedded in the interpretation of the problem is to shift victimization, and the badness attached to it, onto others.

The institutions of justice are, in principle, invested with the power to adjudicate the good. If everything that feels wrong is the result of injustice, then demanding justice is demanding that an omnipotent power fix what is felt to be wrong. In brief, the demand for justice rooted in its omnipotence is a way of externalizing the badness in the self, and the internal seat of judgment that determines where the badness lies.

Past and Present

Embedded in the fantasy of the omnipotence of justice is the search for a power capable of bringing the dead back to life or, at a minimum, countering the evidence that they really are dead and gone. Crystal Fleming (2017) offers an interesting example of this in an article concerning the racist heritage at Harvard University. In the article, Fleming includes, as an example, something that happened there over 100 years ago:

> To take just one example of Harvard's horrors, consider the fact that Charles William Eliot—president of the university in the late 1800s—played a major role in legitimating eugenics, an ideology first developed by white male scientists for the purpose of promoting the genetic erasure of groups deemed to be inferior. Harvard has, in fact, been described as the "brain trust" of the eugenics movement.

For our purposes, what is interesting in the use of this example is that, for Fleming, the past is as alive today as it was a century ago, so that it feels entirely appropriate to include the ideas of someone affiliated with the university in the distant past in an indictment of it in the present.

This collapsing of past and present is an important aspect of survivor guilt, which has the effect of freezing time so that the dead remain present long after they have passed away. The inability to complete the mourning process results in the collapsing of past and present, which means that there can be no future. If there can be no future, there can be no progress toward it, which means that, whatever the claims to a commitment to progress, the real commitment is to holding onto the past, indeed, conserving the past against anyone who might insist we move beyond it.

Implicit in this is an essential aspect of annihilation anxiety already discussed: the movement of the traumatic event from past to present and future. Moving the traumatic event across time holds out the possibility that it might yet be prevented. Guilt, then, organizes and gives meaning to a life devoted to preventing a catastrophe that has already occurred since the same forces that drive the individual to take responsibility for the catastrophe foster the conviction that the individual possesses the power to overcome the catastrophe and erase its consequences by preventing it, in spite of the fact that it has already occurred: "The anxiety of victims is a looming specter: If it happened once, it can happen again. Guilt offers a heuristic which promises control over future negative events: If I act properly, I can avoid persecution" (Juni, 2016, p. 32). Here the tyranny of time plays an important role, as the power imputed to fantasy to overcome temporal limits leads to the substitution of fantasy for reality.

This construction of victimization, guilt, and power supports an ideal of civic engagement grounded in the moral imperative to act in and for the group of those who did not survive. When this happens, guilt, fantasies of omnipotence transferred onto the group, and annihilation anxiety hold the group together. Those who refuse to participate thereby reject the group, especially the guilt-invested fantasy and assumption of omnipotence that binds it together. Of course, feelings of guilt associated with betrayal of the group can foster an intensified attachment to it, an attachment expressed in the intensified condemnation of those outside the group deemed responsible for the damage done to those remaining in it. This intensified attack on those outside the group operates as a strategy for externalizing survivor guilt. At the same time, those who have gained the capacities needed to move out of the group find it difficult to exercise those capacities when faced with the powerful impulse to identify with the damage that holds the group together. When externalizing survivor guilt becomes a significant factor in public life, realistic assessments of the plight of, and meaningful actions undertaken on behalf of, those who have survived are made difficult by powerful identifications and fantasies.

Something along these lines can be observed in the struggle over responsibility for suffering associated with racial identity in the United States. In one case, African-American football players protested inequities, oppression, and violence in society and, particularly, in the criminal justice system by "taking a knee" during the playing of the national anthem prior to games. Doing so was meant to make the statement that the United States was a racist nation. By making this statement, the football players sought to join those living in communities where violence, including violent confrontations with police, created high levels of fear and anger. In the words of the player who initiated the protests, Colin Kaepernick:

> I am not going to stand up to show pride in a flag for a country that oppresses black people and people of color … To me, this is bigger than football and it would be selfish on my part to look the other way. There are bodies in the street and people getting paid leave and getting away with murder. (quoted in Wyche, 2016)

This was an important message about racism, systemic violence, inequality, and injustice. But it was also one offered without any clear connection to any well-defined political engagement having well-defined policy goals, offering in their place a strong emphasis on racism as both the underlying wrong and the factor accountable both for suffering and for defining what must be done to free black communities from poverty, violence, and fear. This suggests that, in addition to the reality-based issue to which attention was meant to be drawn, there was another dimension of the communication, one that was all about the assignment of blame, in other words about to whom guilt would be assigned and therefore who would be bad and who would be good.

As it turns out, several of the football players involved in the protests were, indeed, survivors of the violent environments in which they grew up. Those players who grew up in violent settings had moved out of those communities, most often to get a college education and then to gain employment in a profession that yields an income that, among other things, allows players to reside in wealthy areas, removed from the communities they left behind. These facts also make the possibility of survivor guilt one we should not ignore.

Equally telling was that the protests took place immediately preceding the athletes' participation in a violent sport featuring the enactment of a warlike drama of assault and defense, triumph and defeat. This is a drama that allows no room for ambiguity of allegiance, because allegiance to the group (the "team") is paramount. It is a drama in which the means for achieving the goal is, essentially, repeated acts of violence. The violence featured in the game suggests the significance within the players' lives of violent impulses attached to fantasies of assaulting and being assaulted, of living in a world made up of little other than violence.

The absence of complexity in the game mirrors the destruction of complexity in the protest "outside" the game, where the issue was treated simply as one of the moral failings of a racist nation. No room was allowed for the possibility that the roots of violence could lie in complex connections between sub-national forces both within and outside communities, or for the possibility that relationships between communities, politicians, police forces, and those who have not been victimized (the "privileged") are complex and unlikely to be ameliorated by attributing moral failure to the nation.

Thus, the act of taking a knee did not spark a conversation on the criminal justice system, or even on systemic racism, but on respect for the flag. In the words of one former executive in the National Football League: "What he was trying to spark a conversation about has been muted ... It has been transformed into a debate about patriotism" (Maske, 2017). A debate about patriotism is essentially a debate about group identification, which displaced the debate over what can be done to reduce violence and fear in the black community.

Guilt, Destruction, and the Self

Guilt is the way our emotions signal that we have taken responsibility for ourselves, especially for the harm done to others. In this, guilt is a vital aspect of agency. Agency calls on aggression to defend self-boundaries. Without the capacity for aggression, there can be no assertion of the presence, and therefore existence, of the self. But aggression, whether in the service of the self or not, can have harmful effects. When it does, we may or may not be able to take responsibility for those effects. In other words, we may or may not be able to tolerate guilt. Even when the assertion of self-boundaries does not have harmful effects in reality, there may be such effects in fantasy. As we have seen, this is the case for both bystander and survivor guilt.

A primary expression of the self that comes to be interpreted as an aspect of its capacity for damaging aggression is withdrawal from others. Withdrawal makes it possible for the individual to focus attention on the self and to care for him- or herself. But, separation from others can also be interpreted as an attack on them. When it is, when separation cannot be tolerated by others, and when their expressions of intolerance (which may include aggression) cannot be tolerated, withdrawal into the self becomes problematic (see Bowker, 2016; Levine, 2017). Then, what must be blocked or prevented is making contact with the self and the withdrawal from others—what Winnicott refers to as the "isolation" of the self—that protects the self from relating.

Withdrawal is taken to be an attack when it is interpreted as the statement: "You are not the good." This interpretation implies that those from whom one withdraws deserve to be left behind, an interpretation that, as we have seen, can play an important role in survivor guilt. The implied negative judgment about those left behind makes those who withdraw responsible for the negative judgment of those from whom they withdraw: "Because we withdraw from them, they must be bad."

This makes turning inward and attending to the self an attack, as it was when Colin Kaepernick took a knee. By so doing, he asserted his separation from the group of those who celebrate the goodness of the nation and therefore he asserted that the nation was not good. This did not, however, express his capacity to withdraw from relating and turn toward the self. Rather, it expressed, or attempted to express, his membership in a different group, the one we refer to here as the survivor group. Emotionally, at least, this is suggestive of a return home, if we consider home the place where identification with, or merger into, the group is secured.

If taking a knee had the important consequence of enabling Kaepernick to find his way home, it would be reasonable to assume that embedded in the act was both the statement, "I do not belong here" (i.e. "A racist nation has no place for me"), and the statement, "I wish to return to the place where I do belong," which is the group of those who could not survive, and could not exist, in the racist nation. The statement, "I do not belong here," the associated wish to return to the place where he does belong, and the hidden wish to escape from that place, together constitute a powerful expression of a complex psychic reality that acts as a driver for important political and social conflict. This conflict is organized around survivor groups and the ambivalent attachment of individuals to them.

The wish to return home enacted symbolically as refusal to stand for the national anthem can be considered an expression of guilt for the act of leaving home and going to college, pursuing affluence, and establishing a place in the world outside the group of origin. The guilt may be experienced as the feeling of not belonging when "I do not belong here" really means "I do not deserve to be here." It can also be considered a way of alleviating or preventing guilt, since, according to Kaepernick, it would be "selfish" to stand for the national anthem while others in his community are victims of violence for which those responsible are not being punished. So, not standing absolves him of the guilt of the bystander whose participation in a ritual celebrating the goodness of the nation makes him complicit in the harm done to his home by the nation. And, at the same time, not standing explicitly links him to the survivor group. Thus, even though he remains silent, he is nonetheless speaking out.

The "Guilty Remnant"

An extreme but illustrative example of the rejection of the impulse to go on living, identification with the dead, and externalization of survivor guilt may be found in the HBO television series aptly titled, *The Leftovers* (2017), based on Tom Perrotta's (2011) novel of the same name. The premise of the book and the series is that, on October 14, 2011, 140 million people, two per cent of the world's population, mysteriously disappeared from Earth. Whether those who "departed" were random victims or a "chosen" few, and whether "the departed" have died or have been transported to another place are unknown, and both remain a source of considerable consternation for all.

In spite of its unlikely premise, the show's real focus is the emotional realities of those who are left behind ("left over") and their individual and collective attempts to reconcile themselves with inexplicable loss. Here, Perrotta and the series' writers and directors reveal a degree of sensitivity and insight into the dynamics of loss, guilt, and aggression that illuminate more than one of the issues with which we are concerned. At a social and political level, the catastrophic event, known as "The Great Departure" sparks the creation of a number of cults, some messianic, some apocalyptic, many of which remain unknown to the viewer. The cult the viewer comes to know intimately, however, is of considerable size and boasts multiple chapters across the country: the "Guilty Remnant."

All members of the Guilty Remnant, known casually as the "GR," live together in communal houses, having "left behind" their own homes and families in what is their first, and perhaps most significant, rite of entry. Members sleep on floors and live without material comforts. They destroy all personal possessions, including photographs or heirlooms: anything that attaches them to the lives and persons they left behind. Similarly, they strip themselves of any outward manifestations of personality, choosing their clothing from communal bins or racks where every item is white. All mirrors are removed and windows are covered, such that, in the space established by the group, no member can "see" him- or herself or any other person in the world outside, removing from each member the two most important ways of existing as a person: in oneself and in relation to others. Instead, members can only see other depersonalized members: a constant reminder of the submersion of their individualities and worldly lives into the sequestered, regressed group.

Speaking—perhaps the most basic symbol of the capacity for self-expression—is absolutely forbidden. Instead, members communicate with each other with hand gestures and by writing terse notes on pads of white paper. All must smoke cigarettes—a symbol of morbidity and mortality—a law of which they are reminded by large and prominently displayed placards, reading: "Let us Smoke" and "We don›t smoke for enjoyment. We smoke to proclaim our faith."

The most fundamental tenet of the "faith" of the Guilty Remnant is that the moment of "the departure" was the moment when "the world ended." It is important to note that it is not in any literal sense that "the world ended" on the day of the Great Departure. With 98% of the world's population left intact, governments, societies, and economies still function.

The primary sense in which the phrase "the world ended" holds meaning is an emotional one, and one that takes on meaning at the level of the family. For those like Nora Durst, the loss of the Great Departure was immense. At one moment, her husband and two children were eating breakfast around the kitchen table; in the next moment, all three were gone. But Nora's case is an unusual one; most have not lost entire families, and Nora, herself, rejects the ideology of the GR, so the idea that "the world ended" means something else to its members. The world ended, for those who choose to join the GR, because, at an emotional level, the Great Departure represented something they *already knew*: that one can be abandoned without warning or explanation; that an unknowable force can bring capricious loss; that the world, when conceived as a home, is not a safe place to be.

The external event of the Great Departure, and its recognition by the entire world, then served to confirm an inner reality that members of the GR have longed to have confirmed. Indeed, in one sense it liberated those who would become members of the GR from the burden of living. The Great Departure gave them an impetus or an excuse to act out the dark fantasies and destructive impulses they had long hidden, in attempts to pretend that they did feel safe, that they had not been abandoned, that they do and did find themselves at home in the world.

On this note, it is worth remarking that on the day before the Departure, Patti Levin, the leader of the Mapleton chapter of the GR, is a highly anxious and distressed patient in the care of a psychotherapist, Laurie Garvey. She is there, in large part, because she has suffered years of physical and emotional abuse at the hands of her husband, meaning that her home was, indeed, far from a safe place to be. It is unknown whether Patti's history of abuse reaches back further than her marriage to her childhood, but this possibility should not be excluded. After the Departure, of course, the tables have turned, Patti is strong and confident, and Laurie Garvey is an initiate of the Guilty Remnant under Patti's capable leadership.

If the Guilty Remnant finds its primary mission in being "living reminders" of the loss and destruction wrought by the Great Departure, which is, as we have said, the reality of the destroyed inner world reflected in the loss of safety and goodness in the home, then the GR is, in an important sense, a survivor group dedicated to living death. All their activities are directed toward the end of enacting their own living deaths and imposing living death on others. Although they are silent and do not relate to others in a meaningful sense, they do distribute pamphlets that are headed, "Everything that *matters about you* is *inside*" (in what might otherwise be a powerful statement about the self as the center of experience and meaning). When opened, of course, all the reader finds in the pamphlet is a blank, white page.

They also follow and "watch" outsiders, particularly those who have suffered personal losses. They stand silently, in pairs, outside their homes, confronting these persons with ghostly versions of themselves in their darkest moments of grief and despair. "We watch so they remember," they tell themselves. It is no coincidence that members of the GR occupy spaces near to homes and families, for the home is, as suggested above, the place where the impact of the Great Departure resonates most strongly and finds maximal vulnerability in survivors and potential recruits. The presence (or absent presence) of the GR members at the homes of survivors invites them to recall the destruction of their homes, to give up hope for recovering the ability to "go on living," and to yield to their guilty and victimized selves, which mean to join the ranks of the living dead.

The GR has even adopted the practice of passing out fake (or defused) grenades to outsiders, on which they write the phrases: "Any Time Now" or "Any Day Now." Similarly, one of the placards on the wall of the primary GR encampment reads: "It won't be long now." Exactly what these messages refer to is not clear. On the surface, they appear to refer to the belief, held by GR members and nonmembers alike, that there will soon be a "second" great event, in which those left behind will perish or will otherwise join the departed. Since the fate of the departed is unknown, the possibility of this "second" Departure is both wished for and feared.

Of course, such messages—especially when attached to what, at first, seem to be functioning explosives—represent an extreme and violent provocation, reminding those who have not "died" that their death is, in one way or another, inevitable. Or, if seen as a radical recruitment device, the message may be that those who have not yet internalized the Great Departure as a way of being will inevitably do so, for life outside of the GR—which is to say, life itself—is no longer possible. In either case, the messages seem to be emotional communications of the imminence (and the immanence) of an emotionally catastrophic event that cannot fail to recur precisely because it has already occurred.

There is a remarkable focus on women in the GR, and in the series more generally, a focus it may be helpful to explore briefly in order to understand what is at stake. The vast majority of members of the GR are women, and their leaders, like Patti, seem primarily to be women. The opening scene of *The Leftovers* features a distracted and frustrated young mother struggling with a crying infant in a laundromat, hastily strapping him into his car seat, ignoring his cries as she talks on her cellular phone, and then, suddenly, noticing that he has vanished. Indeed, the very first sounds heard in the series are those of this infant crying: "the human cry."

The dread of losing one's child and the guilt parents of all genders feel for experiencing frustration, anger, or hatred toward their children is, therefore, encapsulated in the series' opening vignette. It is not clear that the mother blames herself, or at least not immediately, but it is clear that she is ignoring the child and, therefore, that she is insufficiently attending to him. This link, then, between the emotional abandonment of the mother and the physical departure of her child is established from the beginning of the drama.

Similarly, Laurie Garvey, psychotherapist and paragon of mental health, is ultimately motivated to leave her family and join the GR because, unbeknown to her husband and children, at the moment of the Great Departure, she loses an unborn child. As she lies on the examination table in her doctor's office watching the ultrasound screen, her fetus—we are not quite certain of its gestational age—simply vanishes; its rapid heartbeat abruptly stops.

Outside of the cult, the link between the Great Departure and maternal failure is equally evident. On a day of remembrance, the third anniversary of the Great Departure, a statue is unveiled in the town of Mapleton which is terrifying in its depiction of a mother either letting go of (failing to hold) her infant child, or of her infant being torn from her arms by an invisible force.

It is as if maternal loss—understood both in the sense of the child's loss of the mother and the mother's loss of the child—were somehow at the heart of the Great Departure and its aftermath. Indeed, it may be said that the two kinds of maternal loss referred to above are always linked, that the child's loss of reliable connection with the maternal object results from and so, is entailed by, the mother's loss of her capacity to connect with, care for, attend to, and protect her child.

Archaic constructions of gender, of maternal ambivalence, and of responsibility for children all help to explain why women seem especially attracted to the message and the activities of the Guilty Remnant. If, as we have suggested briefly above, the destructive element in the Great Departure resonates with inner experiences of maternal ambivalence—which include aggressive impulses directed at children—then joining the ranks of the GR may be a way to defend against guilt by punishing the self (and others). This punishment, not surprisingly, takes forms that mirror parental abandonment, disconnection, and abuse. That is, just as the infant's cries in the opening sequence of the series are ignored, the members of the GR are forbidden to cry. Similarly, just as the statue depicting an infant being separated from the mother's grasp suggests an inability to hold and protect the child, members of the GR live in a setting where their personal needs and desires (and identities) are of no importance, just as they willingly subject themselves to violent physical assault for which they neither seek nor find succor.

There is, of course another—and somewhat more complex—possibility worth considering. If the guilt experienced and endorsed by the members of the Guilty Remnant reflects the operation of a moral defense, then the Great Departure may still be interpreted as a destructive event, but one not sponsored by caprice, cruelty, or even aggression. That is, although perhaps the primary dogma of the GR is that the day of the Departure was the day "the world ended," this "end" may be interpreted in a variety of ways, one of which is as a moment of judgment and salvation, similar to the Christian rapture. If the Great Departure were to be regarded not (or not fundamentally) as an attack on innocence, but, rather, as a moment when a good object—such as "Mother Earth" or a benevolent force or deity imbued with caring, loving, maternal qualities—called "home" her "innocent" children, then it may be possible for some to construe the Departure as an expression of necessity, protection, care, or even love. Of course, if interpreted in this way, those left behind must be guilty, as their assumption of guilt assures that the good object has acted appropriately, righteously, and maternally, and not cruelly or maliciously.

Thus, those who survived the Great Departure, and, in particular the women who make up the majority of the GR, may find themselves (and others) guilty in several ways. (1) They may be guilty for surviving an event that others did not. (2) They may be guilty because, until the moment of the Great Departure, their lives constituted betrayals of their own emotional truth: that, for them, the world had already ended and they were already dead. (3) They may be guilty because the Departure was experienced as an external manifestation (or "revelation") of their own maternal ambivalence and their own maternal failures, which may have included failures of care, love, attention, or protection of children. (4) Or, they may be guilty because guilt alone makes sense of abandonment by the (maternal) good object, whose act can be accounted for, and whose goodness can be protected, if the "remnants" deserved to be left behind. These manifold possibilities and permutations of guilt—and they are not mutually exclusive—help us understand why the Guilty Remnant is so committed to repeating, in different ways, the emotional experience of the Great Departure and why so much of its activity involves the (re)enactment of dramas of penance and punishment, abandonment and death.

In the estimation of the GR, living after the end of the world, that is, surviving the emotional loss it represents, is a betrayal, an attempt to erase or neglect the event and its psychic significance. That is, members of the Guilty Remnant do not act in ways that express the feeling of guilt, at least not directly. Indeed, expressions of feelings of remorse or responsibility for either the Great Departure or for activities conducted as part of the GR are seen as signs of weakness and narcissism, of placing excessive attention on the self. Although guilt is the primary (unconscious) motivation to join and participate in the GR, the real message of the GR is that others are guilty until they join the GR in identifying with the dead.

Members of the GR, therefore, are relentless in their recruitment work, in following and harassing others, and in protesting events, such as "Heroes Day," designed to help survivors heal from the Departure. In the latter case, the GR shows up to the somber and emotionally tense event with a giant letter-board sign that reads: "Stop Wasting Your Breath." This demonstration, of course, provokes a violent onslaught by attendees, and many GR members are injured. Indeed, the police find themselves in the somewhat awkward position of having to defend the psychologically terrorizing group from citizens who have lost themselves to blind rage.

At one point, the GR orchestrates an elaborate plot to manufacture costly and lifelike mannequins to "replace" all those who were lost at the moment of their departure, such that survivors like Nora Durst, for instance, walks into her kitchen one morning to find, at her breakfast table, three lifeless, life-sized dolls, molded and dressed to look exactly like her husband and children. The shock and grief this action causes culminates in a riot that injures many GR members and burns their communal houses, but these reactions to provocation do little to stop the activity of the GR; indeed, they are part of the design.

One reason the GR succeeds even when it is attacked is that its actions are designed specifically to provoke intense rage and hostility in others. The greatest aggression is provoked, of course, not in residents who have found healthy ways of going on living in the wake of tragedy, but in those who have denied, repressed, or sought to forget the event and its emotional meaning. For them, the mere presence of the GR is indeed "a living reminder" of a psychic experience of self-destruction, to which most people respond with aggression.

Being both provocateurs and recipients of aggression are important parts of the mission of the GR for two reasons: (1) Suffering harm and aggression allows members of the GR to be beaten, spat on, struck, and violated in ways that speak to the unconscious need for punishment as a member of the survivor group of "the Guilty." (2) Provoking aggression is in keeping with the GR's mission of thwarting others' access to the emotions and activities that would permit mourning and the restoration of the capacity and desire to go on living. That is, by acting aggressively toward an ostensibly passive object—GR members do not fight back, cry out, or verbally respond to assault—the individual is invited to identify with and occupy the role of the aggressor against a lifeless object. In doing so, the individual is set at odds with, or prevented from access to identifying with, his or her victim self. Instead, he or she makes contact with his or her victimizing self and its limitless, destructive rage.

In attacking a member of the GR, the individual finds him- or herself attacking a stand-in for the object or objects lost in the Great Departure, and for what they represent: the loss of a family and a home. Thus, those who attack members of the GR are pulled into the fantasy world of the GR, and of survivor groups more broadly, where they find themselves acting out a role of destructiveness linked to their need to defend their own self-boundaries. Their presence of self comes under attack by the GR in the form of continual provocation, and when they defend themselves, they find in themselves a destructive force perhaps all too familiar to that force of self-defense that may come to be linked to the destruction of the home and the family.

For having defended him- or herself and unleashed aggression, the individual feels guilt and, so, even at the moments when an individual may wish to express an adamant rejection of the "Guilty Remnant" by using physical force to push them away, the individual also confronts his or her own guilty self and, in that sense, comes one step closer to leaving her home and joining the ranks of the living dead.

CHAPTER NINE

Privilege

The idea of privilege has lately taken on importance in the attempt to assign responsibility for deprivation and suffering. In academic literature, popular culture, and mass media, the meanings attached to the term "privilege" vary. They range from more or less factual accounts of the social and economic advantages certain groups have been afforded to something deeper and more complex. These deeper and more complex meanings possess a moral quality in which the privileged party is burdened with guilt for undeserved advantages received (or potentially received). The privileged individual or group is deemed guilty because the logic of the current discourse of privilege dictates that having benefited from privilege is morally equivalent to having created and supported the social system that privileges certain groups over others.

The term "privilege" typically refers to "a right or immunity granted as a peculiar benefit, advantage, or favor" (*Merriam-Webster's Collegiate Dictionary*, 2006). In the recent rhetoric of privilege, emphasis has been placed on the way a benefit becomes a privilege when it is unearned. Thus, in speaking of privilege, Peggy McIntosh asks herself the question, "What do I have that I didn't earn?" (Rothman, 2014). In this way of thinking, the unearned benefits referred to by the term "privilege" are most often linked to being a member of a favored group (Sehgal, 2015).

In one usage, privilege is simply a descriptor for benefits linked to inherited attributes. Thus, McIntosh describes the matter in the following way:

> What I believe is that everybody has a combination of unearned advantage and unearned disadvantage in life. Whiteness is just one of the many variables that one can look at, starting with, for example, one's place in the birth order, or your body type, or your athletic abilities, or your relationship to written and spoken words, or your parents' places of origin, or your parents' relationship to education and to English, or what is projected onto your religious or ethnic background. We're all put ahead and behind by the circumstances of our birth. We all have a combination of both. And it changes minute by minute, depending on where we are, who we're seeing, or what we're required to do. (Quoted in Rothman, 2014)

Race is a circumstance of birth and not a personal achievement. So, if we have benefits because of our race, those benefits constitute privileges understood in this way, and members of a racial group in an advantaged position can be said to be privileged in relation to members of other racial groups. Gender operates in a similar way, at least so far as gender is taken to be assigned according to anatomical characteristics rather than gender identifications chosen or achieved. Even, however, if we consider neither race nor gender to be the results of physical endowments, they can still constitute groups the members of which enjoy unearned benefits. The point of speaking of privilege as a birthright, then, is to emphasize that the benefits accruing to members of a group are not rewards for the achievements of the group or of its individual members.

Ta-Nehisi Coates (2012) describes a set of benefits unconnected to physical characteristics that he associates with privilege in the following way:

> In short—you need to know that I was privileged. I can run you all kinds of stats on the racial wealth gap and will gladly discuss its origins. But you can't really buy two parents like I had. Money can buy experience and exposure—but it can't make you want those things. It can't make your parents curious about the world. It can't make them moral, compassionate and caring. It can't make them love their children. As I have moved on up, in that old Jeffersonian sense, I have seen families who allegedly were more privileged. But ultimately I find merit in who they are as humans. I am unconvinced that money trumps all of their flaws.

You cannot buy your parents, nor can you be said to earn them. You do not earn a family where education is valued and your parents are well situated to support and assist you in learning. You do not earn a family that provides a nurturing environment, one where management of difficult emotions is assisted, where the kind of love that prevents destructive emotions from dominating is available, or where a positive emotional investment in the self is not overwhelmed by feelings of guilt and shame. None of these benefits is earned; yet all are vital, and they all can play a part in determining what the individual is able to achieve in his or her life. The privileges to which Coates draws our attention are essentially part of an environment that is either there for the child or is not.

Agents and Beneficiaries of Privilege

The passive construction of privilege in most definitions is worthy of note. Privilege is "granted"; advantages are "received" or "enjoyed." Nevertheless, as Coates' account suggests, privilege implies not only the receipt of unearned benefits, but the presence of a subject who made things the way they are (who granted, gave, or awarded them), with the result that certain advantages would be enjoyed by some and not others. We might assume that the subject who grants privilege is a group of those who are, themselves, already privileged, whose members act individually or through institutions over which they exert control. But this is not the assumption made by those lately drawn to the rhetoric of privilege. For them, the distribution of privilege is not the result of a set of conscious and deliberate actions taken. It is not, or not primarily, the activity of powerful agents—in the form of individuals or groups—who grant benefits or impose deprivation. Rather, privilege is something hidden outside of the awareness and conscious intent of "the privileged."

The trend toward the use of the term where an agent empowered to grant privilege is absent is exemplified in the following statement (McIntosh, 1988):

> Through work to bring materials from women's studies into the rest of the curriculum, I have often noticed men's unwillingness to grant that they are overprivileged, even though they may grant that women are disadvantaged. They may say they will work to improve women's status, in the society, the university, or the curriculum, but they can't or won't support the idea of lessening men's. Denials that amount to taboos surround the subject of advantages that men gain from women's disadvantages. These denials protect male privilege from being fully acknowledged, lessened, or ended.

McIntosh does not mean to limit her point to male privilege, but to apply it more broadly: "I was taught to see racism only in individual acts of meanness, not in invisible systems conferring dominance on my group." Should we conclude that these "invisible systems" are the agents who grant privilege to some while denying others? And if they are, and if they are "invisible," then how can we understand why and in what ways they exercise their agency, and how can we effectively "acknowledge," "lessen," or "end" the problem of privilege? Does not the current construction of privilege mystify it and thereby make it harder, not easier, to identify and address real problems of inequality, discrimination, and violence?

One might argue that there are complex "systems" and "cultures" with normative features that, in effect, determine and distribute privilege. To these systems and cultures, we might strive to attribute an agency, although the nature of the agents and their actions is so amorphous as to make them unknown and, very likely, unknowable. But, more to the point, to say as much is to contradict what has become a fundamental tenet of the contemporary discourse of privilege, which is to confer guilt not on the "invisible" agents who confer privilege but, rather, on the recipients of privilege, holding them responsible for enjoying benefits in whose distribution they had no part.

Central to grappling with this question is the answer to the related question: Can it be said that the deprivation of some implies privilege for others, as McIntosh insists when she asserts that "men gain [advantages] from women's disadvantages." The answer is clearly yes if the deprivation is decided on and enforced by those others, if it is taken by them as an exclusive right. In a slave society, for example, slave owners enforce slavery. Similarly, prior to passage of the 15th Amendment to the US Constitution, white Americans (or those white Americans empowered to decide) deprived black Americans of the vote. And, prior to passage of the 19th Amendment, men deprived women of the vote. So, voting was a privilege.

But, is the answer to the question posed above—"Does the deprivation of some imply privilege for others?"—still yes, when no discernible decision or action prevents others from enjoying similar advantages? That is: Can there be privilege without agency? And can there be agency without any overt or conscious power to exercise it? If there cannot, what is the exact meaning of the assertion that those with unearned benefits—benefits that have not been in any way overtly bestowed—are "privileged?"

If there is an active agency responsible for conferring privilege, it remains hidden. It is, in the language introduced above, "invisible." If we accept this premise of an agency outside of our ability to see or know it, then we can only come to know of its presence from an examination of its effects, which is, in short, to confuse cause with effect. Therefore, the differences in benefits, advantages, comforts, and other goods that we see in society seem to provide all the evidence we need that those who receive unequal or underserved benefits are also responsible for dispensing privilege, depriving others, and sustaining the "system" in which such dispensations and deprivations are realized.

The Privilege of Home

While the idea of responsibility in the absence of any action or conscious intent may be difficult to credit, if we consider unconscious mental processes, the matter of attribution of responsibility, without conscious intent to deprive, can make sense. To see how this might be the case, we need to consider the role of fantasy and especially of the archaic object relations expressed in it.

Concern with archaic object relations naturally leads us to consider the quality of early childhood experience. Coates emphasizes the unearned benefits he received as a result of being in his family, insisting that these are benefits money cannot buy. They are, instead, the benefits that accrue to those whose parents provide their children with a safe place to be, a space—a home—that nurtures the development and expression of talents, interests, and the capacity for a positive emotional connection with self and others. This home environment is the place where a parental connection can become, through internalization, a safe space in the inner world. If having this safe inner space is a privilege—perhaps the most important privilege—then those who are not so privileged find themselves in a family environment that is not a safe space for self-development or a place in which they can explore possibilities of being and doing not already determined by ascribed identities. When the absence within the family of a safe space for this exploration is internalized and then projected outside, it fosters the experience of living in an unsafe world. Living in this unsafe world makes it difficult to form the kinds of relationships with others that sustain the process of the development of capabilities in line with interests and talents: to learn and mature in ways conducive to making a life of personal achievement and satisfaction.

Of special importance in thinking about privilege is the experience of parental love, not as an environmental given, but as something contingent on behavior that indicates to the child that he or she deserves it, as an earned rather than unearned benefit. Then, the facilitating environment is experienced as a privilege, and those who have access to it are considered to be privileged, as they have been granted an unearned benefit of childhood, which is also the epitome of all unearned benefits.

We experience the availability of a benign inner world as a privilege when we experience parental love as something we must earn, while others take it for granted. This difference is the starting point for the idea of privilege in its current usage, since it is what makes parental love an unearned benefit in the eyes of those who did not receive it, or for whom love was made conditional or contingent. The problem is that if you cannot take parental love for granted, but must earn it, it ceases to be parental love; and the environment created by the parents turns into a dangerous place, a place where love may easily be lost and where something else may be found where love ought to be. The invisibility of privilege, then, resides in the fact that we don't know where to find it. And, we don't know where to find it because we have, of necessity, hidden it from ourselves. Specifically, we have hidden from ourselves the source of our own deprivation of love and the implied deprivation of the opportunity to internalize a benign or safe inner world.

These considerations may illuminate the following statement on privilege attributed to Kristen Tea (2017):

> I want my friends to understand that "staying out of politics" or "being sick of politics" is privilege in action. Your privilege allows you to live a non-political existence. Your wealth, your race, your abilities, or your gender allows you to live a life in which you likely will not be a target of bigotry, attacks, deportation, or genocide. You don't want to get political, you don't want to fight because your life and safety are not at stake.

The ability to live in a safe world is here described as privilege. And, of special interest, the unsafe space in the world outside to which we refer above is identified with "politics." But, of course, those who are not privileged are not required to, or forced to, participate in politics; in other words, they are not required to live in the dangerous world of politics, and indeed most of them do not, although the circumstances in which they find themselves may cause them to suffer danger or harm or to otherwise live in ways that put them at risk. And, yet, while Tea is not compelled in any obvious way to involve herself in the dangerous world of political engagement, she still feels that she has no choice. And, she feels that she is owed something by those who do have a choice. Her insistence, if taken seriously, can tell us something important about the matter of privilege.

Of special interest for our purposes is the way Tea treats politics as a dangerous space on a par with the spaces in which members of racial or gender groups sometimes face dangers at work or on the street. What connects the two spaces is that those in them feel that they have no choice but to engage in "struggle." This suggests that, in both spaces, the struggles engaged in have something important in common: the factor that compels engagement, that is, the "invisible systems."

We might begin to understand better this matter of invisible systems if we consider another term close to it, a term we consider earlier in the context of our discussion of speaking out: silence. McIntosh (1988) uses this term when speaking about the invisible systems, thereby indicating that the term invisibility also refers to our silence about them:

> To redesign social systems, we need first to acknowledge their colossal unseen dimensions. The silences and denials surrounding privilege are the key political tool here. They keep the thinking about equality or equity incomplete, protecting unearned advantage and conferred dominance by making these subjects taboo. Most talk by whites about equal opportunity seems to me now to be about equal opportunity to try to get into a position of dominance while denying that systems of dominance exist.

If we consider this statement more closely, what is most striking about it might not be the claims it makes about privilege, but the four words with which it begins: "To redesign social systems." The "we" for whom the author speaks in making her statement is the group of those who are in the business of designing social systems, a group to which she assumes or imagines that she belongs. Most people, of course, do not consider themselves members of this group, and for good reason. If we were to be more accurate, then, we might say that the first person plural used to address those for whom the author speaks is the group of those who imagine themselves to be in the business of redesigning social systems. In other words, it refers us to a fantasy about the self.

Where McIntosh insists on agency, most people feel they have none. But, for her to assume that they are wrong, even that they are in a state of self-serving denial, about the matter, is for her to take for granted something that is far from self-evident. Nor is it at all obvious that, as some would argue, agency is always there for the taking, so that the reason we don't have it is that we don't take it, and therefore that power resides in our ability to speak out, should we only be willing to do so.

Most adults, in so far as they live in an adult world, do not find that saying something makes it so. And, indeed, it is the loss of the conviction that speaking out has this power that marks the transition to adulthood and the "silence" implied by it. Still, it is not unreasonable to insist that, *if* saying it makes it so, then acknowledging—speaking out about—privilege might release those who have none from their deprivation. And, if that were the case, not speaking out—remaining silent—could be considered the reason that the needed change does not take place.

Tea speaks about privilege in the language of choice: the choice to withdraw from struggle, which is the choice to remain silent. Her claim is that remaining silent about injustice empowers it. As it turns out, even if this is a problematic statement about the relationship most people bear to the way the world is, it is also, in its way, an accurate statement about the inner world, which is a world not of action, but of thought, a world in which what is not thought exerts the most powerful influence, a world in which the greatest struggle is the struggle for hegemony over what is thought. At the center of this struggle is the quality of self-experience, which is determined by the quality of the thoughts we have about ourselves. So far as this is the case, whether our internal voices speak out for the self, or are silenced by other voices that speak against it, becomes, in its way, a life and death matter.

Once silenced, the self becomes invisible, or, in Winnicott's term, "hidden." When the struggle over the hegemony of thoughts about the self is projected outside, others are subsumed into it. But, for them, the terms of the struggle are reversed. Their struggle is to unleash the voices within that attack the self, the voices that represent guilt and shame. By speaking out against themselves, the privileged would free others to speak out for themselves, which means that the failure of the privileged to speak out against themselves is the reason others are unable to fend off the invisible power responsible for their self-hatred.

The whole struggle over privilege then becomes a struggle over who will bear the burden of guilt. And, the whole point of insisting that those who are "privileged" take responsibility for the plight of those who are not is that by taking on guilt they will relieve others of it. If we then consider the real burden at the heart of the struggle over privilege to be the burden of guilt, it follows that privilege is imposed by what is *not* said by those who are imagined to have the power, through their use of words, to relieve the guilt of those who do not have privilege. We might also say that the primary purpose of the rhetoric of privilege is not so much to assign blame as it is to secure innocence, which, of course, can only be done by assigning guilt to those who are not innocent. The use of the term privilege, then, moves us onto the terrain of the moral defense rather than the plane of reality-based assessment of the forces that determine the situation in which individuals and members of groups find themselves.

This suggests that we consider the absence of choice, especially the choice to opt out of the struggle, not as something imposed from outside, but as a compelling quality of the inner world. The absence of choice would be, then, an aspect of the hegemony in the inner world of forces hostile to the self, which is the seat of choice and the factor within the personality whose presence in doing and relating makes choice meaningful. When the external containers for the factor internal to Tea's personality responsible for the attack on her self refuse to relieve her of her burden, the outside world becomes the source of her suffering, and her internal struggle is externalized. The world becomes a dangerous place in which her only option is to struggle against the self-destroying forces found there. She must involve herself in the dangerous world of political struggle because to fail to do so is to confront her internal struggle and the internal sources of her feelings of shame and guilt.

For Tea, then, privilege means freedom from the internal struggle, something we can only have if our inner world is not a dangerous place to be. By contrast, those who are free from the kind of inner struggle to which we have just referred are so not because of the power of projection, but because they have been privileged enough to internalize a benign inner world. And they have been able to do so because of the availability during their childhood of parents who provided a safe space or facilitating environment. This is, indeed, an unearned benefit, which makes it that much more difficult for those who don't have it to tolerate living in a world with those who do. Insistence on privilege is, as Coates suggests, a powerful statement of something real, something that may or may not be provided to us. When it is not provided, the experience of seeing it provided to others can provoke intense emotions. Then, the term becomes a powerful lament for something not only lost but taken away: the safety of the world of the family and consequently the safe space of the inner world.

The attack on privilege at the societal level has focused on the idea that privilege constitutes an injustice, with the implicit and sometimes explicit insistence that, if any lack privilege, none should have it. Yet, a challenge posed by the use of the term "privilege," where there is no discernible agent granting unearned benefits, is that, if those benefits are not granted and yet exist, there is no injustice implied in their existence. For injustice, there must be agency. The absence of agency in accounts of privilege and in similarly construed discourses of inequality, then, undermines the effort to understand difference in modern society as a matter of justice and injustice.

Where norms and laws respect equal access and equal opportunity, and where protections against inequality, discrimination, and violence are in place—and they are all too often absent—the reference to injustice is best understood as a lament about the inner world and the loss of a facilitating environment referred to above. Blame here is transferred from the failed archaic object to those outside, to those experienced as the recipients of the care denied to those who lack privilege. At the unconscious level, projection fosters the belief that others were granted significant emotional benefits of which we were deprived. Then, these benefits are, indeed, unearned.

Privilege and Achievement

The unearned benefit of a facilitating environment is just that: the benefit of an environment that facilitates the healthy development of the inner world of the child. Although that environment does facilitate, it does not directly produce the life outcomes of those enabled by it. The outcomes we associate with a healthy home environment, then, are not privileges. Success in the development of the capabilities associated with maturity and self-determination is still an achievement of the person, as are the accomplishments of life lived once the individual internalizes, and therefore moves outside of, the facilitating environment afforded in the object relations that make up family life. But the more we interpret all life outcomes as the result of privilege or its absence, the less they can reasonably be thought of as achievements. Indeed, insistence on privilege is an attack on the idea of personal achievement, which is the idea that outcomes express the presence in the individual of a good or worthy self, a self that is embodied in good works: accomplishments that reflect favorably on those responsible for them. At the same time, reference to privilege can be a way of insisting that those who have failed bear no responsibility for their failure. Rather, success and failure are understood as gifts or favors bestowed on some and refused to others.

Contemporary use of the term privilege is meant to deny or take away achievement from those who are capable of it, and to replace pride in achievement with penance and self-negation in the form of guilt for depriving others. If you succeed in making your life your own, this achievement is at least partly the result of actions you have taken, actions for which you are responsible. But, within the rhetorical world of privilege, your achievements are not the result of your work and talent, but of your privilege. They are not achievements.

In some ways, the whole privilege perplex arises because one person's pride is seen as the cause of another's shame. If others take pride in their accomplishments, but we cannot take pride in ours, then we feel diminished by their achievements. This dilemma, refracted through the prism of subjective causation, translates into the idea that those who take pride in important aspects of their lives cause others to feel diminished, or even less alive, such that the purpose of their achievement and the presence of their selves in their lives is to impose shame on others. If those who do not have privileges do not have achievements, they become bystanders. They are forced to watch from the outside, unable to participate in the shaping of their own lives. Making achievement a privilege deprives ourselves of achievement as much as it deprives others.

Privilege and Groups

One way to defend the self against shame is for those who are deprived to take responsibility for their condition, thereby turning shame into guilt. As we have discussed, guilt is a painful emotion, but because it results from taking responsibility, it appeals to the presence within the individual of the capacity to make doing an expression of an internal factor, whereas shame expresses passivity that results from the failure of the internal source of action. Better to be responsible for your condition (active) rather than shamed by it (passive). Taking responsibility need not be, and presumably, in most cases, is not, a conscious decision, but an unconscious conviction that coexists with its opposite held at the conscious level. But, even so, it expresses the presence, or wished-for presence, of agency.

Recourse to guilt as a defense against shame becomes more plausible where formal legal protections of rights are in place, but significant differences in opportunity according, for example, to gender or race, remain, so that outcomes appear to reflect failures internal to groups rather than deprivations imposed from outside. The use of guilt as a defense, which operates primarily on the individual level, can be turned into a group or social defense through projection of responsibility for failure to achieve onto those who occupy putatively privileged positions. The idea of privilege, then, becomes part of an attempt to assign responsibility for the failure of achievement on the part of those who fall short of a social-cultural or group ideal when there has been no overt granting of benefits.

The attack on the idea of achievement embedded in the rhetoric of privilege is linked directly to a central feature of that rhetoric: insistence that the individual be subsumed into the group and that his or her putative achievements be understood simply as privileges claimed by the group. In recent literature on the subject, the whole matter of privilege is formulated in the language of group identity. This way of formulating the problem has its roots in the insistence that benefits received are unearned, which means that they are disconnected from the self. Then, if the individual receives benefits that have nothing to do with his or her unique presence of being, or what is distinctly individual about him or her, they must have something to do with shared characteristics or qualities and the way those qualities are made the reason the individual receives special benefits.

Thus, foremost among the responsibilities of the privileged, as those have lately come to be understood, is the act of confessing one's privilege—if not publicly, at least to oneself. In this confession, the confessor acknowledges that he is stuck in his group identity, that he can never be, say, nonwhite, and that he must always bear the burden of the identity marker of whiteness with which he was born. Here we may discover the real purpose of accusations of privilege, which is to instill in the privileged person or group a psychic dilemma that is similar to that of the underprivileged person or group: to be "stuck" with a group identity that one did not choose and to be painfully conflicted about loving and hating that group. Here we are not speaking about love or hatred of a race or gender, but, rather, about love and hatred for the part of the self that identifies with the group. Of course, this conflict between love and hate is defended against in different ways, perhaps most commonly by insisting that one is "proud" of one's group identity and that it is only other people (i.e. the oppressors) who use social and cultural privilege to cause the self and the group to feel anxiety and shame.

The Privileged and the Condemned

It can be fairly said of Albert Camus that the essence of his *oeuvre* is rhetorical attack on the abandoning or depriving agent. As we have now alluded to more than once in this book, Camus rails at "the world" and at God for not being present, for not responding to our needs, for not bestowing on us what we need to make our lives worth living (see 1955, pp. 2–15). In this sense, Camus' work is also about privilege, the privilege of feeling "at home" in the world and the experience of being denied this feeling.

Those who believe they are at home, for Camus, have lied to themselves. They have taken an unjustifiable "leap of faith," or have otherwise betrayed a truth they know or ought to know about life and about themselves: that human beings can never be "at home" in the world. Those who claim to be at home are the privileged who provoke rage and envy for enjoying a comfort we lack. With only a few exceptions (see 1995), Camus wrote of this privilege not in a literal sense, but in a broader, philosophical one.

In Camus' most famous novel, *The Stranger* (1988), the main character, Meursault, delivers a speech that attempts, in part, to articulate the privilege of being at home and its falsity or baselessness. Meursault directs his tirade against the chaplain who comes to visit him before his execution:

> What did other people's deaths or a mother's love matter to me; what did [the chaplain's] God or the lives people choose or the fate they think they elect matter to me when we're all elected by the same fate, me and billions of privileged people like him who also called themselves my brothers? Couldn't he see that? Everybody was privileged. There were only privileged people. The others would all be condemned one day. And he would be condemned, too. (p. 121)

Earlier, we asked how the "invisible" objects associated with the bestowal of privilege can be understood, and, indeed, whether our preoccupation with them might mystify the issues the rhetoric of privilege seems intent on clarifying. One problem with raging against invisible, abandoning agents or missing feelings of home is that virtually all that remains of such objects is held in fantasy. Thus, hatred of the abandoning object and envy of the privileged who have not been abandoned becomes self-hate, and the position of one who rages against the impossibility of being at home in the world—a position embodied not only in Camus' "absurd stance" but in much late modern and postmodern thought, at least since Nietzsche and likely well before—comes to resemble the position of the melancholic who finds himself stuck in a "mental constellation of [perpetual] revolt" (Freud, 1917e, p. 248).

As Freud put it, when "the shadow of the [lost] object [falls] upon the ego" (p. 249), the abandoned self punishes itself along with the object to which it is now bound or fused, finding a certain pleasure in identifying with the pain-inducing qualities of the object and even in suffering the pain inflicted on the self. Thus, in revolting against the unjust distribution of privilege, one ends by becoming and enacting the role of the abandoning or depriving object one rejects.

CHAPTER TEN

The Broken Family and the Destroyed World

Relationships and Groups

We speak of a relationship when a connection exists between two persons who are, in some sense and to some degree, separate, so that there also exists something of themselves outside the connection. For a relationship to emerge, it is not necessary that the connection between the parties be freely chosen by them, although that is one possibility. Still, without some involvement of subjectivity, there is no real participation in the relationship. To participate is to enact the relationship, to do the things that establish its existence, and, in some sense, to commit oneself to it. The specific kind of action tells us what kind of relationship the parties create together.

A group, by contrast, exists when what is created by the parties to a relationship endures even if one party no longer participates, which can only be the case where there are more than two participants. It might seem that the group's capacity to sustain itself in the absence of one or more of its participants places it at an advanced point along the axis of social and emotional development, more advanced than both the relationship and the primitive dyad that precede it. However, as Wilfred Bion has emphasized, this may not be the case (1961, pp. 188–189). Instead, it may be that the group represents powerful tendencies toward regression away from relating and toward a more primitive state of being. When this is the case, the goal of the group is to overcome the differences that separate persons, differences whose preservation marks their connection as a form of relating. In other words, the purpose of groups of the kind just considered is to overcome the conditions that make relating both necessary and possible, so that a more primitive state can be attained, or, at least, that the hope to attain such a state can be kept alive.

The more primitive state is marked by the availability of a maternal object having the capacity to receive the child's communications (of self-states) and to manage the emotions in them, so they can be made tolerable. Communication of this sort assumes and insists on the inclusion of the maternal object in the emotional world of the infant. This inclusion assures that the infant will find himself in a safe space where he can exist.

By contrast to this state of inclusion, relating is something that happens between two separate centers of emotional experience. Yet, relating, in its most primitive form, means identification: the "earliest expression of an emotional tie with another person" (Freud, 1921c, p. 37). Identification finds or creates sameness in difference. What makes identification different from the primitive dyad are the limits required if the two parties are to retain their separate existence, even as they are linked by the bond of identification. The movement from inclusion in a single emotional experience to identification with a separate center of emotional experience is a movement from what is experienced by the infant as an undifferentiated unit to a relationship.

The transition to the world of relating is also a transition to living in the family properly considered. This transition does not occur all at once. Rather, the primitive connection continues to exist as an important part of mental life, making regression a possibility even as relating takes up more and more emotional space. The same logic applies when we think about groups and the pressures that move individuals and families away from relating and toward group experience. The possibility, indeed likelihood, of regression in emotional life means primitive emotional states continue to play a significant role even in adult life, notably in group settings.

For those groups whose purpose is to suspend the members' need to relate as separate individuals, the group is also a way to obviate any need to participate, at least in the sense of participation used above. This is because the purpose of being in such a group is to rid the world of separate subjectivities. Without separate subjectivities, there can be no issue of deciding to enact a relationship or deciding not to do so. Indeed, there is no meaningful sense in which enacting a role is a possibility, as there exists no discernible entity capable of acting. Were we to ask, or even insist, that people actively or meaningfully participate in such a group, we would be asking them to participate in a setting that allows for no participation. In other words, we would place them in a double bind. It follows that, in so far as our political system is meant to be experienced as a group process of the kind just considered, the demand that people participate is a demand that they sacrifice their capacity to participate.

Being and Belonging

For the individual, participation has its original meaning in the family, where it refers to occupying a role and enacting the ideas and fantasies that make up family life. Among these ideas and fantasies, one of the most important is the one centering on participation itself. This is a fantasy about belonging, both belonging to the family, and the family's belonging to a greater unit: possibly an ethnic, racial, cultural, religious, or political group (a political party or a nation). Three alternatives are of special importance: (1) The family may define itself as a group that belongs to a larger group; (2) The family may define itself as a group that does not belong; or (3) The family may define itself as something other than a group.

In the second case, we can begin to see how the family might be structured as a survivor group: a group that survives in a hostile world where it does not belong. The question of participation in the family arises only in the third case, when the family conceives itself as something other than a group. Instead, the family conceives itself, or strives to conceive itself, as a network of relationships. Although the family conceives itself in this way, the powerful bonds that hold families together, such as attachment and shared experiences, remain in effect. But, in this case, these bonds can be suspended, temporarily or permanently. They may even be broken. Family members can refuse to participate and yet remain within the family, where struggles may ensue over participation, but where banishment from the family or collapse of the family is neither a threat nor a likely outcome.

There are both centripetal and centrifugal forces operating in families. Families come together, and they come apart. A family that does not conceive itself as a group becomes a more secure family—secure in the sense that the family can draw on, rather than reject, family members' differences and individualities. The secure family draws active and robust participation from its members, and the family is a safe place for members both to be (themselves) and to belong (to the family). At the same time, the outside world, which, particularly but not exclusively for children, is interpreted according to the schemas and patterns set by family life, will be experienced similarly: not as a hostile place where there is no room for the individual, but as a place where it is possible both to be and to belong.

The more the family conceives itself as a group, the less secure the family, and the more ambivalent will be the attachment of family members to it. Here we speak of "ambivalent ... attachment" not strictly in the sense of attachment styles set out by John Bowlby (1971) and his students (see Ainsworth et al., 1978)—although these classifications may be relevant—but in a broader sense, in which the attachment of individuals to the family and to specific family members is marked by ambivalent emotions: particularly by love and hate, by desire to belong to the family (group) and resentment that such belonging requires a suppression or loss of being or presence.

In sum, when the family conceives itself as a group, the conflict between being and belonging cannot be overcome, and the fate of the individual in the family/group is necessarily "tragic," as Alford puts it (1994), because in such family experience, something must always be destroyed or lost. In this condition, family members, and the family itself, will find a need to make use of projection to cope with problematic aspects of family life. Individuals, groups, organizations, and institutions outside the family will come to contain split-off or intolerable emotions, assuring an ambivalent attachment to them.

A family may suppress relating and participating so that it can be constituted as a group. If it does, the constitution of the family as a group operates as a defense against the threat of dissolution of family ties. The more powerful the regressive forces in the family, the less stable it is as a family, since the demand for relating implicit in family life threatens the hopes (of security, identification, and unbreakable attachment) embedded in the regressive pull of primitive emotional states. Regressive forces that work to turn the family into a group dismiss the imperative that family members *develop*; hence, the "hatred of development" to which Bion draws our attention (1961, p. 89).

Turning the family into a group would make it a vehicle for retrieving and preserving the more primitive maternal connection. The greater the influence of that connection—or, more precisely, the greater the influence of the fantasy of being capable of retrieving it—in shaping the meaning of family, the more the family will abandon or reject its function, and its obligation, to create a space conducive to the development of children (and adults) who can thrive away from the family by autonomously engaging with the world outside.

Broken Homes, Broken Families

The home is the instantiation of the family in physical and emotional space. The home is also a transitional space in which forward and backward movement can occur as part of a developmental process. The capacity of the family to exist in multidimensional space depends on the degree to which the family members have internalized the safe space, which in turn depends on the degree of safety provided in the family. Those who have are not driven by the need to use others to contain their emotional states (Winnicott, 1958b, p. 32). "Going home" is a complex and important fantasy in emotional life, especially as it represents, in physical space, the return to a more primitive mode of connection, and regression to a form of dependence involving a special feeling of safety. Similarly, the feeling that "we cannot go home"—or, as Thomas Wolfe put it (1940), that "you can't go home again"—suggests the inevitable loss of something vital in maturing and living.

Internalization of the maternal connection moderates the need to return home either literally or figuratively, just as the failure to do so intensifies that need. But there may not be a home to return to, a situation that may be due to the same factors that limited the internalization of safe space. Then, the desire to return home is a desire to return to a fantasy of home, a fantasy that can express the impulse to repair the faults in the home that impeded the internalization of a safe place in the inner world and that empowered disruptive or dangerous forces in family life. In this case, the sought-after repair of the damaged home is also the sought-after repair of an inner world that has no safe space in it, no space where it is possible for the individual to find him- or herself.

A second, related, fantasy, is one of replacement rather than repair. In this fantasy, rather than repairing the home, a new, undamaged, home is created or found. Living in the new home will feel right and good, and, because of this, will dispel all the troubling feelings provoked by life in the old home. One important consequence of preoccupation with the fantasy of replacing the damaged home is that, rather than making us safer, it has the opposite effect.

Home is the place where you will find the family. If there is no home, the family can only be found in hopes, dreams, and memories. Any event in the life of the family that separates the family from its home has the potential to threaten the family unit. Separating family members from home can be the result of the normal emotional development of the child. Because the maturation of the child can challenge and diminish the home, the child may experience him- or herself as the source of the disruption of the safety it provides. This taking responsibility for disruption of the primitive emotional connection can then extend to responsibility for disrupting the family and damaging the home.

But damage to the family can also result from events other than the normal development of the children in it, events such as divorce, loss of dwelling space, illness or death of a family member, and emotional withdrawal on the part of one or both parents. Some of these events are unique to the particular family, while others express larger events in the external world: unemployment, war, immigration, shifts in the social-cultural meaning of marriage and divorce, changes in the norms of work and child care that limit access to parenting, and so on.

The sense of belonging for family members is undermined when the family loses its home, whether that loss takes place in physical or emotional space. The loss or breaking of a home may be a literal loss of a place to live, or it may refer to the psychological destruction of the connections that hold the family together.

Members of a broken family may go their own way, seeking to find or create in the world outside a new and intact family. But, when they do, they carry with them an important residue of the broken family: a special kind of hope that replaces a natural expectation of safety and connection that develops when the home remains intact to a sufficient degree during childhood. This means that the new family will carry a special burden: It must fulfill a fantasy of familial connection shaped by the kind of failure that marked life in the older familial setting.

Hope and Survival

The hope to which we have just referred is, in important ways, similar to the hope involved in the survivor syndrome. Both are hopes that something lost will yet be found, that, in this sense, death is no definitive rupture in the vital emotional connections of family life. The more this hope shapes relationships in the new family, the more we can expect that family to exhibit features we associate with survivor groups. When the family becomes a survivor group, the enactment of relationships between family members involves the loss they share and the feeling of damage associated with it.

One result of damage done to the family is that the family drama can move from one of belonging in the larger world outside the family to one of rejection both by and of that world. An important characteristic of survivors is their refusal to have a life in the world when those who did not survive cannot. When, as a result, the world outside becomes, or is experienced to be, a threat to the family of survivors, rather than a supportive environment for it, that world becomes a source of damage to the family that weakens or alters the attachment of members to it. There then develop parallel processes involving refusal to participate at both levels, so that refusal to participate in the world outside can become the defining feature of interaction and attachment within the family.

In a sense, when the family defines itself as a unit that refuses to belong to the world outside, its emotional life is not fundamentally about *what* the family refuses to belong to, but about its refusal to belong, *tout court*. Failure of the family to be a place where it is possible for the member to be can be enacted in the relation between the family and the world outside, so that the latter is experienced as a dangerous place. When this happens, the family is all about the celebration of its outsider status, which holds it together as a unit and makes it special. But, of course, this makes everything outside the family suspect.

Use of the world outside to contain the disruptive forces internal to the family can lead to the experience of the outside world as a chaotic and dangerous place, and to actions on the part of family members that make the outside world more dangerous to them, so that reality better mirrors fantasy and better serves the emotional needs of members to externalize responsibility for trouble within the family. In those cases where the damage to the family has its cause outside in larger, institutional, or systemic processes, cause and effect are merged, so that the family and the world outside are simply two stages on which to enact the same drama.

The organization of the family around the theme of survival can promote the attachment of family members to those groups outside the family that also embody the survivor mentality. These groups reject not this or that aspect of the larger social-political world, but everything about that world.

Thus, those groups that identify "the system" as what they reject implicitly make rejection an end in itself. For them, any participation in—which is to say, having a life in—the larger world represents acceptance of it and, therefore, betrayal of the family and of the ethos of the broader survivor group whose terms now shape attachment to the family. This is betrayal in both senses: It betrays (reveals) the family secret—which is that the family is all about rejection and loss—and, in refusing to be bound by a life-denying role in the family drama, it betrays (violates) the code of the family itself.

The word "system," as it is used here, refers to a setting in which people relate on a nonfamilial basis. This system is an "outside" world that emotionally represents the damaged internal world and the failure of the home to be the safe place it is wished to be. In the words of Christopher Lasch (1995), what lies outside the home is a "heartless world," from which the home offers a "haven." But the family may not be the sought-after refuge from a heartless world if the family has suffered damage, especially due to its relationship with the world outside. If the family lacks the capacity to offer safety and comfort, this lack creates a powerful impetus to experience the outside world, or "the system," as the enemy of the family. "The system" is constructed in fantasy through projection of the dark reality of the family as part of a strategy to preserve the hope that a good, safe family can be rebuilt.

If the family rejects all avenues for making a life outside the family and in "the system," it radically limits the possibilities for self-expression and creative living for its members. It makes the world outside a reflection of a dark inner world, shaped by internalization of a family system organized around the negativity of damage. In this case, the impulse to live in the outside world, whether acted on or not, provokes the guilt associated with betrayal of the family's constitutive fantasy. This is where survivor guilt becomes an essential element. Survivor guilt is a mechanism by which the individual is prevented from making a transition from life in the family to life in the world outside, at least life of the kind that involves any genuine emotional investment in and attachment to living in that world.

It is important to bear in mind that, in families organized as survivor groups, doing harm to the family is a necessary part, and a necessary role, in the family drama, and not a challenge to the meaning or definition of family life. Rejection of the family enacts the central element in the mental life of the family organized as a survivor group. The difficulty of the task facing the individual who would separate him- or herself from the family survival drama is evident in the necessity that to break emotionally with the family is not simply to reject it, but to overcome responsibility for doing so, or, more precisely, to free oneself from the guilt associated with the harm assumed to result from rejection. The individual's act of rejection is not the real source of the harm done to the family, but, rather, a strategy employed by the family to hide that real source by enabling it to identify and blame scapegoats within the family.

Faced with such a family situation, the only way for the individual to have a life is to leave *and* to overcome the guilt provoked by leaving. Doing so requires that the individual overcome, or at least minimize, identification with the survivor group. This means that leaving home may not signal the moment of freedom from the family survival drama, but the continued enactment of it. Those who leave may do so to enact their role as the cause of damage to the family. They may depart with little more than the hope of finding new families of fugitives, castaways, or outlaws to join. When leaving takes on this meaning, guilt becomes a primary element in shaping what the individual does in the world outside and in determining the kinds of attachments available to him or her there.

Compliance and Attack

For those who grew up in families organized around survival, participation means playing the designated role in the survivor group, and, since participation means attachment on the basis of survivor guilt, participation tends to fit the individual best for membership in survivor groups available in the world outside the family. Yet, for reasons considered earlier, participation in survivor groups is not real participation to the extent that it depends on the sacrifice of self-determination. This problem is further highlighted when we consider that an important dimension of playing a role in these groups is compliance, which is to say, hiding the self. Activity expressive of the presence of the self (self-determination) indicates the presence of a person, existing in his or her own right, and not as a vessel for the enactment of dramas scripted by the demands of group life. There is a sense, then, in which compliance, because it withholds from the group any genuine involvement or commitment, expresses refusal to participate in the most basic sense of the term.

When living in the world means compliance, what appears to be participation is actually the withholding of the self from engagement, and therefore, nonparticipation. This nonparticipation reflects the disengagement of the self from the family (a) to protect the self from what is experienced as a dangerous place to be, the home, and (b) to protect the family from self-expression, which is understood to be a fundamental threat to the family's integrity. Paradoxically, what most often makes the home a dangerous place to be is the threat to the integrity of the home attributed to self-expression there.

Compliance, as a way of hiding the self, and therefore as a strategy for nonparticipation, can be driven by the attachment of guilt to the self for its role in the destruction of the family or for making the home something less than a home. Because of this, we expect to see compliant behavior dominate in survivor groups, including those devoted to rejecting "the system" and refusing to live in it. This is, indeed, the case for political groups devoted to "systemic change" yet intolerant of any changes that fall short of the complete overthrow of established institutions and norms. Thus, the US Congress, led by the Republican Party that was bent on ridding the country of a "hellish law" (the Affordable Care Act), insisted we should "repeal and replace" it, aggressively rejecting the possibility of revision and repair.

Indeed, in politics, the combination of compliance and radical attacks on existing institutions indicates that issues of survival predominate, and that the engagement expressed in group attachment is part of the strategy to disengage the self. The self-expression that poses a threat to the family is another term for the impulse to "go on living" in a world where others did not, considered more fully in Chapter Seven. To counter this impulse to go on living, the living identify with the dead, and even act out deathly attacks on life-sustaining institutions and organizations rather than separating themselves from them.

The Immigrant Fantasy

Just as the westward migration carries with it a number of complex issues concerning broken families, homes lost or left behind, and fantasies of rebuilding or creating a new, safe place to be, the contemporary debate over immigration offers an especially apt metaphor for the hope that a broken home can be replaced by a new one. The fantasized replacement, because it is new, would be undamaged and, therefore, capable of providing the safety and nurturance unavailable in the home of origin. A nation that sees itself as a destination for immigrants because it is, itself, a "nation of immigrants," is a nation organized emotionally around the broken family. Such a nation imagines immigrants as members of broken homes, and because of this, immigrants represent broken families as well as the hidden truth of those presumably settled families whose members have become citizens. In other words, it may be that the central problem immigration poses to citizens is that it confronts them with their own broken families and damaged connections, both internal and external. Hostility toward immigrants indicates the power of denial that our families are broken and enacts our need to disavow feelings about ourselves and our families.

Advocacy of immigration in language such as, "Everyone is welcome here," suggests the need to enact a family drama involving repair of damage to the family using others and their families as surrogates. It expresses the fantasy of the nation as a "home" in the "heartless world," a message vividly expressed in the Emma Lazarus poem, the last part of which is engraved on a plaque on the Statue of Liberty. The poem describes the statue, and more generally the nation represented by it, as "a mighty woman with a torch, whose flame is the imprisoned lightning" and whose name is "Mother of Exiles":

"Keep, ancient lands, your storied pomp!" cries she
With silent lips. "Give me your tired, your poor,
Your huddled masses yearning to breathe free,
The wretched refuse of your teeming shore.
Send these, the homeless, tempest-tossed to me,
I lift my lamp beside the golden door!"

The statue stands at the entrance to a nation personified as a fierce mother who calls out silently to those cast out from "ancient lands," a phrase that conjures archaic relationships torn apart, families broken and homes lost, lands that falsely celebrate a decaying order.

The powerful symbolism begins with the powerful maternal image, both defender and personification of the lost home. This depiction of the immigrant's destination as the replacement for a lost home, together with the personification of the nation as "mother," suggests its relation to the complex connection between home and family discussed earlier. The more the home is needed to fill in for the lost or broken home, the less fully safe space has been internalized, the more the new home is identified with the maternal object. This tendency to equate home with maternal object is important because it makes damage done to the home damage done to that object, just as it makes aggression felt toward the maternal object aggression directed toward the home.

Throughout most of history, the maternal object has also been a mother in the narrow, sex- and gender-specific sense of the term. The attack on the integrity of the home, then, in so far as it is an attack on the maternal object, is also an attack on the gender traditionally associated with mothering. When, as a result, women are identified with the maternal object, what damages women also damages the maternal connection and, therefore, the home. Perhaps of greater importance, whatever hostility emerges in the home in response to its failures and limitations is hostility directed toward the maternal connection and, by extension, toward women. And this is the case whatever the gender of the family member experiencing hostility toward the family. It follows that in the nation of immigrants, we are likely to find significant, if often hidden, hostility and even hatred directed at women.

But as aggression directed at the maternal object and toward the home are not easily tolerated, in large part because they provoke excessive guilt, these attacks on the maternal object and the home must be displaced onto those who would invade our home and destroy the maternal object it represents. In this way, the fierce mother embodied by the Statue of Liberty is a symbol both of protection and safety, and of a maternal object who failed to create for us a safe home, that is, a mother whose inattention, neglect, or incapacity to provide a safe space would have provoked in us the kind of guilt and aggression with which we have been concerned throughout this book.

Thus, while the poem suggests the playing out of a drama of a maternal connection lost and found, there is another side to the immigrant fantasy. This is the side represented by Donald Trump when he describes immigrants as a danger to the nation:

> When Mexico sends its people, they're not sending the best. They're sending people that have lots of problems and they're bringing those problems. They're bringing drugs, they're bringing crime. They're rapists and some, I assume, are good people, but I speak to border guards and they're telling us what we're getting. (Kopan, 2016)

It is as if, for Trump, the Statue of Liberty is a fierce mother who defends the nation (family) against the threat posed by those who would cross its borders, rather than offering protection for those who have nowhere else to go.

Advocacy of draconian measures to restrict immigration indicates, among other things, the need to avoid confrontation with an internal reality represented in the immigrant: the reality of abandonment, disruption of vital family ties, loneliness, and the intense aggression fostered within that reality, especially toward the maternal object. In the anti-immigrant rhetoric, themes having to do with the responsibility of the immigrant for damage to *our* family (the family of those who are native to the country) are common, as exemplified by insistence that immigrants take jobs away from citizens.

As Trump emphasizes, the immigrants we do not want are those who are poor, who come from poor and damaged countries. The effort to keep immigrants out can be an effort to keep alive the fantasy of the security and love provided by the nation as an intact family, and especially as an intact maternal connection. At the same time, willingness to break up families by deporting some family members but not others transfers our own disrupted family experience onto others, insisting that our experience of a broken home be shared. The struggle over immigration policy may not be so much a matter of dealing with threats to national security or cultural identity as it is a matter of the emotional significance of the disruption of family life and the loss of a secure place to be (the home).

Thought about in this way, the political drama surrounding immigration policy can be considered a way of managing our feelings about ourselves as aliens in our own homes, occupants of the role of disrupters of family connection, and representatives of the theme of rejection of family life in survivor families. The intensity of the need to protect national security and cultural identity reflects the intensity of the feeling that the home is under attack, which, in turn, suggests how powerful are the internal disruptive forces in family life, including those associated with survivor guilt.

To the extent that guilt predominates in the inner worlds of those whose families have been broken or whose homes have not afforded them a safe place to be, we may say guilt forges identifications with immigrants and with homeless children, identifications which are uncomfortable if not intolerable, and are subject to repression, denial, and externalization. The individual who finds him- or herself in this psychic position—a child without a home—is, in an important sense, blocked in his or her trajectory of personal development, stuck in the maturation process that leads from childhood to adulthood. The (real and imagined) child in such a situation is unable to create a new home and is, at the same time, unable to stave off or repair the catastrophic loss and damage that has already occurred. This is the child who awakens alone, in a new and unfriendly world, described in Chapter Two.

What can be done is to move toward a fantasized new world and away from a broken family whose memory one wishes to erase but whose basic contours are repeated endlessly in the grown-up child's enactments. These enactments seek to impose the destroyed inner world onto others in the (false) hope of building a new world, a new home, and a new family that will be bound together by shared loss, the suppression of the self associated with the family that conceives itself as a group, and, most importantly, the imperative that all members of the new family identify with their guilty selves.

Conclusion

A child awakens in a new world. What is new about this world is both absence and presence: the absence of those who are familiar and the presence of those who are not. This world in which the child must relate to people he does not know (strangers) is the world sometimes referred to as "civil society," although it goes by other names as well (on civil society, see Levine, 2011). Some use variants of the term "liberal" (e.g. "neoliberal") to refer to it, although this term no longer bears a precise and agreed-upon meaning. Others use variants of the term "capitalism," although that term refers only to the aspect of civil society involved with the production and distribution of private property. For our purposes, what is essential about civil society is that it is the world of the *self*-made life, of the boundaries set by respect for individual rights and private property, and of a robust sphere of personal responsibility and self-determination. It is a world in which we are, in certain important respects, on our own and required to take care of ourselves. Contract, rather than care, defines relationships in civil society.

A problem arises for the child who awakens in this world when he or she is not prepared to live there. Some would argue that *no* child is prepared to live in civil society, indeed, that no person ever could be. For those who advance this argument, civil society is condemned because the lack of care for us on the part of others is its defining quality. For some, this makes civil society a dubious enterprise, a "heartless world" governed by soul-destroying institutions. Because civil society is not a space in which we will be cared for and attended to in the way we were cared for in the old world, civil society comes to be equated with the world born in the aftermath of the destruction of the old world. For the child, being in civil society becomes, emotionally if not logically, the *consequence* of the destruction of the family. In the fantasy with which we have been concerned, civil society does not coexist with family life. That is, civil society is not a part of the world that awaits us after our time in our family of origin has ended, when we mature to the point of independence. Rather, it is an alternative world where family ties have been broken and cannot be repaired or replaced.

Now, there are two (fantasy) worlds: In one world, we are cared for; in the other, we must care for ourselves. For the child who inhabits this second world but is not prepared to live there, *surviving* is the best he or she can hope for. In the new world, the only alternative to an existence organized around survival, "bare life" (Agamben, 1995), or "barely being" (Bowker, 2019), is to search the new world for whatever remnants of the old world can be found there, or to attempt to build a facsimile of the old world out of materials available in the new.

There is, however, in fantasy at least, also a third possibility: a world outside the family that is not a civil society. An important twentieth-century fantasy about such a world is described in George Orwell's classic, *Nineteen Eighty-Four* (1949). Orwell's novel was heavily influenced by the Soviet system, which, on one level, was an experiment in creating a new world that was neither family nor civil society. The Soviet system arose from and depended on the destruction of civil society. It aspired to create a family-like world outside the family, a family of the whole, a collective being. The effort to escape civil society became the effort to build, in its place, a communal utopia that turned out to be driven not by familial bonds, but by the fear of living in a world of strangers and an intensity of aggression directed at the freedom of movement and self-determination that such a world affords.

In keeping with the language used throughout this book, we can say that there is a configuration of the inner world organized around the dilemma of being unprepared to live in civil society. In this configuration, the self, which is the moving force the individual must call upon to live in civil society, does not feel safe there. It does not feel safe because safety is equated with the availability of the secure environment for the self afforded by the presence of its good objects. The absence of these good objects provokes aggression directed against them, aggression from which they must then be protected.

To cope with this situation, the good objects must be enclosed within a psychic fortress, where they will be safe from the violent internal objects conceived in the mind to give shape to aggression. Put another way, the aggression directed against good objects and against the self that exists in their presence is the same force that imprisons them.

In Chapter One, we considered how this configuration of the inner world is represented in the drama of *Godless* as the struggle against the outlaw gang that roams the destroyed world. At the same time, the need to safeguard the self and its connection with (lost) good objects is well-represented by Charlotte Temple, the owner of La Belle's hotel. Temple foreshadows the town's final confrontation with Frank and his gang in an early episode where she reveals that her hotel, where the women of the town will take refuge from the gang's anticipated assault, was deliberately constructed out of "brick and iron" in order to make it impossible to burn down. If we recall that the characters in *Godless* represent figures in the inner world, then we can read the ultimate battle scene as a depiction of rage against good objects (the maternal figures in the town, the women of La Belle) on the part of their lost children (the outlaw gang). We can also see the lengths to which one will go to protect these good, maternal objects: building a fortress (the hotel) where they will be secure.

But, if the good objects must be imprisoned in order to be protected, the world can only become a cold and heartless place, with no remnant of the good in it. Because of its dependence on the connection with its good objects, the true self cannot exist in this world. Just as the good objects must be kept secure by their imprisonment in a fortress, the true self must be hidden, and a false self put in its place (Winnicott, 1965). The false self protects the true self by mobilizing aggression against the impulse to make contact with the true self and express its presence in doing and relating. The result is that civil society becomes a world defined by the pursuit of the ends of the false self. Although civil society is meant to be the place where adults are self-determining, the greater the involvement of civil society with the false self, the less space available there for real self-experience and real self-determination.

The Necessity of Guilt

So far in this Conclusion, we have discussed two options for coping with or escaping from life in the "new world" of strangers: (1) the communist or pseudo-communist utopia, which is also a dystopia, or (2) inuring oneself to life in a heartless world by walling off the true self and living as a false self in a false-self system. But there is a third option, which is the one we have explored in this book: the formation of a guilty self. The guilty self makes those who embrace it a healing presence in the destroyed world. Indeed, the act of becoming the guilty self is meant to heal the world and to do so without banishing the self from it, at least so far as it can be said that the self is the prime mover in its own subjection to its healing mission. There is, in the hope embedded in this balancing act, an effort to keep the self alive and present, but only in endlessly repeated acts of self-denial, just as the (lost) good objects are kept alive only by preventing any connection with them.

The processes just summarized are embedded in Orwell's novel. There, we observe the imposition of guilt on those who would free themselves from totalitarian rule. Specifically, the subversive manifesto attributed to the hated heretic and Resistance-leader Emmanuel Goldstein turns out to have been written by an Inner Party government committee, with the apparent intention of articulating an alternative understanding of events that is seductive enough—and descriptively accurate enough—to tempt individuals to commit thoughtcrime. These individuals will then be captured, tortured, and ultimately made to assume responsibility for the destruction actually created by the state. This means that, even within Orwell's highly politicized narrative, we see clearly the importance of guilty selves as necessary or constituent parts of the fantasy of the destroyed world, a brutal world of desolation and absence that is nevertheless blamed on the presence of figures whose expressions of self and of noncompliance with group (the Party) norms perpetuate the drama of eternal conflict between good and evil forces.

In Orwell's imagined society, guilt is necessary because guilt fosters a group fantasy of the "Fall" of humankind that is linked to the expression of the individual's separation from, or rejection of, the group that demands that it be experienced as the good object. In the Christian version of this fantasy, the good object has come to Earth to save us from our bad selves. Indeed, the good object becomes the victim of our destructive impulses. We destroy that object (in fantasy) and forever carry the burden of guilt (sin) for doing so. In other words, we internalize our destruction of it as a vital part of becoming a guilty self. Guilt for the expression of autonomy—the ability to live separately from the good object—binds people together in a community of faith in that object. This faith proclaims that, if we are good, the good object will return to us, or we will return to it. At the same time, the power of self-determination deemed responsible for the loss of the good object finds expression in the internalization of the relationship with the good object in the form of a fantasized personal connection with God.

Psychoanalysis offers a secular version of the process of internalizing the good object, with the important difference that, in psychoanalysis, internalization is treated as something that develops out of a relationship not with a fantasized entity, but with a real person. This makes internalization not a decision to do or believe the "right" thing, but an alteration in the configuration of the inner world. In the newly internalized relationship, the harsh attack on the self that defines previously established internal object relations is not reproduced but replaced by a relationship with an empathic object.

The relationship with the empathic object features presence rather than absence, understanding rather than judgment, particularly an understanding of what is unacknowledged and judged unacceptable in the personality. It is this relationship, the essence of which is understanding, that weakens the hold of guilt rooted in the feared power of aggression to destroy the good object. In other words, it is the capacity of a *new* object—the analyst—to survive the patient's aggressive attacks and to remain available as a source of empathic connection that alters the configuration of his or her internal object world in a way that alleviates the power of guilt there.

Internalization of an empathic relationship does not, and is not intended to, free the individual from all experience of guilt, but only to free the individual from the experience of guilt associated with the conviction that he or she is essentially bad. Freedom from this conviction makes it possible to acknowledge guilt associated with real harm done to others, and therefore makes possible the kind of reparation that relieves feelings of guilt. It may even be said that internalization of the good object makes possible feelings of guilt for real harm done, just as taking on the badness of the world impedes feelings of guilt for real harm done, since, in the latter case, all guilt is experienced as an indicator of the intrinsic badness of the self and the definitive loss of love that implies.

By contrast, the object relation based on the willful attachment to the good, to the extent that it makes dominance by the bad self the premise for relating to the good, makes identification with the bad self a condition for connecting with the good. If selfhood is perceived as a threat to the society, community, or group, then agents of the group will take it to be their responsibility to insist on the essential badness of the self in order to defend the pride (essential goodness) of the group. Such defenses both mistake and disguise the way attacks on the self undermine the individual's capacity for authentic activity. And such relationships between groups and their members do not reduce the power of guilt in the psyche, but, instead, entrench that power by insisting on it as the basis for relating, thereby reinforcing the suffering the power is intended to alleviate. They do so by affirming the essentially destructive power of the self and by insisting on the need for rigid control if the individual is to be prevented from further destructive attacks on the good.

Psychic Integration and Loss of the Capacity to Think

We need to bear in mind that the tragic drama of the self discussed here is fueled by a single, constituting experience: the experience of the child who is unprepared to live in the new world and yet must somehow manage to do so. As we note above, some would argue that no child can be prepared for the catastrophe he or she must endure. Yet, in part at least, this judgment is validated by nothing more than the insistence that it is true, an insistence fueled by the fantasized experience that has been the primary subject of this book.

So far as what we know about the external world, and therefore what we can imagine to be possible there, is wholly shaped by what has been true for us—which is the truth of the appropriation in fantasy of our own experience—then it is inevitable that we will conclude that being prepared for life in the new world is impossible. This conclusion, which expresses our inability to *conceive* such a possibility, is not surprising if we understand what sets limits on what we can conceive. If we cannot conceive the possibility of being prepared for life in the new world, it is because we are not prepared; and we are not prepared because we have insufficient experience of a process that would prepare us: the internalization of the good object relationship. As a result of a premature disruption of this process, our way of relating in the world tends to express both aggression against it and defenses against that aggression. But when we relate to the world on this basis, we act in ways that assure we will find it a dangerous place, as is clearly the fate of Frank Griffin and Roy Goode in the drama of *Godless*. This means that we find ourselves in the "closed system" to which Ronald Fairbairn draws our attention (1958).

When the closed system becomes the shape of the world in which we live, then it is true that the options laid out above for coping with the new world are our only options. But our insistence on the inevitability of the closed system is nothing more than an attribute of that system, which is a system in which only fantasy objects exist and nothing else can be conceived. Another way of saying this is to point out that the closed system depends on acceptance of the simultaneously self-refuting and self-validating principle that truth must be contingent on belief. This principle does not hold if there are, or, more precisely, if there can be, another kind of truth, which is to say another kind of object in the mind, an object that does not take the form of fantasy (Levine, 2017, p. 18).

How do we know that the creation of this other kind of object is possible? And how does that possibility bear on the possibility of living in civil society? In thinking about these questions, we might consider more closely the events described in Orwell's novel. Once captured and convicted, the protagonist, Winston Smith, an Outer Party member who nevertheless harbors doubt about and hatred for the Party and Big Brother, is not summarily executed or exiled, but is subjected to an elaborate process of torture and brainwashing. The purpose of his torture is to eradicate in him the capacities for autonomous thought, judgment, and action that we associate with self-determination, capacities the availability of which determine whether or not we are prepared to live in civil society. Only after he has been "converted" and "reshaped" (1949, p. 251), "squeeze[d] ... empty and … fill[ed] with ourselves [the Party]" (p. 253), will his torment come to an end. Only after all subjective and authentic impulses (including the impulse to know and tell the truth), and only after he makes what will seem to him to be an accurate confession of all of his crimes (most of which he has not committed in reality), will he be released and, most likely, put to death.

Taken as fantasy, what does this process of "brainwashing" represent? Clearly, it represents the breaking of the individual's connection to external reality. But it also represents the individual's disconnection from his or her own reality, which connection forms the basis for connection with others and therefore with external reality. In the novel, the individual is disconnected from the reality of cause and effect, of action and outcome, and (especially) of harm done and responsibility for it.

What Orwell describes is an experience that fragments the psyche, that "crushes" the individual "to the point from which there is no coming back," when "everything will be dead inside" the individual (p. 253), eliminating his or her capacity to contain and integrate internal experience. The disruption of the ability to integrate internal experience then impairs the capacity to integrate external experience, which is the capacity that makes external objects something real *in the mind by* forming or conceiving representations of them: internal objects that are not shaped by fantasy.

Central here is the capacity to conceive or construct a special internal object—the self—not as a fantasy, but as something *real.* It is no accident that O'Brien attacks this special object directly, insisting to Winston not only that his memories of himself and others do not exist, but, even more fundamentally, that "you do not exist" (p. 257). Only in so far as we can exist, in a real sense, can we conceive other selves not as external emanations of our fantasies, but as objects existing in their own right and therefore as *real* things. Our ability to do so is the *sine qua non* of our ability to live in civil society, which is a space where other persons—persons we do not already know because they do not already exist for us as internal objects—come to exist for us in forms distinct from the forms taken in fantasy.

If we are able to read the torture fantasy in *Nineteen Eighty-Four* as something more than an elaborate condemnation of totalitarianism, we will see that it depicts a relationship and a process through which the capacity to form a connection with both internal and external reality is disabled. What, then, can we say about the nature of this relationship and this process (torture) that deprives us of the capacity to conceive of life in civil society?

The Greatest Fear

What we know about the torture in Orwell's novel is that the torturer, O'Brien, has access to his victims' minds and that he uses that access to identify the victims' greatest fears. For Winston, this fear is embodied in rats. Winston has recurring nightmares in which rats both are and are not hiding behind a dark wall. He knows they are there but is unable to face them and seems to awaken himself if they threaten to make their presence known

(p. 145). There are, in the novel, several suggestions that this nightmare is a dream about the loss of his mother, for whose death he feels responsible, since she disappeared at the moment when Winston (as a child) had run away from home, after stealing his sister's chocolate ration. It is not unreasonable to speculate that Winston's guilt for his selfish act coalesced both with his survivor guilt and with the agony of losing his mother, his family, and his home.

Indeed, it is not unlikely that when the young Winston did return to his home, and therefore to the traumatic absence of his mother and family, in their place he might have found a rat or a pack of rats, as rats are "everywhere" in the world of the novel. Even in Winston's secret room where he meets (illegally) with his lover, Julia, a rat invades their sanctuary and their peace (p. 145).

In the torture room, starved rats are affixed to Winston's face in a cage whose small doors, if opened, will permit the rats to bore into his eye-sockets or mouth and therefore both literally and figuratively get inside, or inhabit, him. This is what is intolerable: that the most dreadful thing, that which contains everything bad and toxic in the world for Winston, including his own guilt, will become him, or he will become it. This helpless confrontation with rats and all they represent is, for Winston, a fate worse than death. In the end, Winston realizes that the only thing, the only "body," he can thrust between himself and the rats is that of his lover, so, in a tragic betrayal, he screams: "Do it to Julia! Not me! Julia! I don't care what you do to her. Tear her face off, strip her to the bones. Not me!" (p. 282).

These facts about Winston's torture tell us something important about the relationship and the process that will, for the individual, sever his or her connection to reality. First, the torturer can only know the content of the victim's mind if the torturer exists in the victim's mind, in other words if the torturer exists not as an external but as an internal object. For Winston, "O'Brien was a being in all ways larger than himself. There was no idea that he [Winston] had ever had, or could have, that O'Brien had not long ago known, examined, and rejected. His mind *contained* Winston's mind" (p. 253, *emphasis in original*). It can even be said that it is the presence of the torturer in his or her mind that the victim most fears. And, since activation of the inner torturer severs the individual's connection with reality, it is that severing of connection that is the victim's greatest fear, whatever the specific form the imagined torture takes for the particular individual.

In the specific case in the novel, the torturer enters Winston's mind through the vehicle of the rats who threaten to gnaw their way in, and, by so doing, threaten to become the sole content of his inner world. This is also the process by which the torturer becomes the victim's dominant internal object, as fear-invested fantasies of rats and of torture involving rats destroy the victim's good internal objects and take their place. Most notably, the rats replace Winston's mother by consuming the internal good object that she represents. They also induce Winston to betray the one person who comes closest to representing a maternal, loving object in Winston's life (Julia), who cares for and loves the unique expression of his self, without regard for his deviation from the laws of the Party. It may also be worth noting that this betrayal of Julia seems to be the torturer's aim, as it represents the victim's willingness to abandon or destroy the connection with the good object (or its surrogate) in favor of surviving in a guilt-ridden and desolate world. After he utters his betrayal of Julia, Winston hears the cage doors close.

That this process of destruction of the good object is one of "gnawing" and "devouring" suggests how primitive the process is and how early in Winston's emotional development it is set in motion. And, because the torturer already exists in the victim's mind, as does knowledge of the victim's greatest fear, it would be reasonable to conclude that the event the prospect of which provokes the greatest terror in the individual *has already occurred.* Otherwise, how would the victim know it? We have, of course, adduced our own example of this from the drama of *Godless*. Our example is Frank Griffin, who knows his own death. To the extent that we can consider this example an archetype, we can use it to pin down the object of our greatest fear not as that takes form for the particular individual, but more generally. Our greatest fear is expressed in the experience that produced in Frank the conviction that he knows his own death, as it did for Winston. This is his experience of the violent severing of all connection with his good objects, a severing that left him alone in a dangerous world.

To take the matter one step further, and to emphasize once again that we are dealing not with experience in the external world but with fantasy, we may say that this severing of connection is the severing of connection with internalized good objects. More precisely, it is the disruption of the process of internalizing the good objects *before* they can be fully instantiated, when the individual depends on their actual presence and the availability of a relationship with them. This disruption creates the loneliness we associate not with the absence of other persons in the (external) world, but with an inner world bereft of comforting objects and object relationships.

The success of relationships and processes that resemble Orwellian psychological torture, in other words, is inversely related to the strength of the internal good objects as measured by their ability to fend off attack. And, the strength of the good objects is commensurate with the strength of the nurturing relationships available to the child and on whether those relationships persisted long enough to complete the process of internalization. When internalization of the good objects fails, we cannot feel safe relating to others, or connecting to our selves. Then, what is most to be feared is not any external danger that looms before us, but the terror associated with dwelling in the mind, which has become a place dominated by the endless repetition, in fantasy and memory, of a drama of destruction.

References

Abdel-Nour, F. (2003). National responsibility. *Political Theory, 31*: 693–719.

Agamben, G. (1998). *Homo Sacer: Sovereign Power and Bare Life*. D. Heller-Roazen (Trans.). Stanford, CA: Stanford University Press.

Ainsworth, M., Blehar, M., Waters, E., & Wall, S. (1978). *Patterns of Attachment: A Psychological Study of the Strange Situation*. Hillsdale, NJ: Edward Erlbaum.

Alford, C. F. (1994). *Group Psychology and Political Theory*. New Haven, CT: Yale University Press.

Alford, C. F. (2002). *Levinas, the Frankfurt School, and Psychoanalysis*. Middletown, CT: Wesleyan University Press.

Alford, C. F. (2009). *After the Holocaust: The Book of Job, Primo Levi, and the Path to Affliction*. New York: Cambridge University Press.

Arendt, H. (1998). *The Human Condition* (2nd edn). Chicago, IL: University of Chicago Press.

Baldwin, J., & Mead, M. (1971). *A Rap on Race*. Philadelphia, PA: J. B. Lippincott. Selections reprinted in: Popova, M. (2015). https://www.brainpickings.org/2015/03/19/a-rap-on-race-margaret-mead-and-james-baldwin. Accessed March 12, 2018.

Balint, M. (1969). *The Basic Fault: Therapeutic Aspects of Regression*. Evanston, IL: Northwestern University Press, 1992.

Bataille, G. (1985). *Visions of Excess: Selected Writings, 1927–1939*. A. Stoekl, C. R. Lovitt, & D. M. Leslie, Jr. (Trans.). Minneapolis, MN: University of Minnesota Press.

Bataille, G. (1988). *Inner Experience*. L. A. Boldt (Trans.). Albany, NY: State University of New York Press.

Bion, W. R. (1961). *Experiences in Groups*. London: Routledge.

Blackman, L., Cromby, J., Hook, D., Papadopoulos, D., & Walkerdine, V. (2008). Creating subjectivities. *Subjectivity*, *22*: 1–27.

Bollas, C. (1987). *The Shadow of the Object: Psychoanalysis of the Unthought Known*. New York: Columbia University Press.

Botting, F., & Wilson, S. (Eds.) (1997). *The Bataille Reader*. Oxford: Blackwell.

Bowker, M. H. (2013). *Albert Camus and the Political Philosophy of the Absurd*. Lanham, MD: Rowman & Littlefield.

Bowker, M. H. (2014). *Rethinking the Politics of Absurdity: Albert Camus, Postmodernity, and the Survival of Innocence*. New York: Routledge.

Bowker, M. H. (2016). *Ideologies of Experience: Trauma, Deprivation, Failure, and the Abandonment of the Self*. New York: Routledge.

Bowker, M. H. (2019). *Misinterest: Essays, Pensées, and Dreams*. New York: Punctum.

Bowker, M. H., & Levine, D. (2018). *A Dangerous Place to Be: Identity, Conflict, and Trauma in Higher Education*. New York: Routledge.

Bowlby, J. (1971). *Attachment and Loss—Volume I, Attachment*. London: Penguin.

Butler, J. (2004). *Precarious Life: The Powers of Mourning and Violence*. London: Verso.

Camus, A. (1955). *The Myth of Sisyphus and Other Essays*. J. O'Brien (Trans.). (First Vintage International Edition.) New York: Vintage.

Camus, A. (1956). *The Rebel: An Essay on Man in Revolt*. A. Bower (Trans.). (First Vintage International Edition.) New York: Vintage.

Camus, A. (1988). *The Stranger*. M. Ward (Trans.). (First Vintage International Edition.) New York: Vintage.

Camus, A. (1995). *The First Man*. D. Hapgood (Trans.). (First Vintage International Edition.) New York: Vintage.

Caruth, C. (Ed.) (1995). *Trauma: Explorations in Memory*. Baltimore, MD: Johns Hopkins University Press.

Caruth, C. (1996). *Unclaimed Experience: Trauma, Narrative, and History*. Baltimore, MD: Johns Hopkins University Press.

Carveth, D. (2001). The unconscious need for punishment: Expression or evasion of the sense of guilt. *Psychoanalytic Studies, 3*: 9–21.

Coates, T.-N. (2012, April 27). White privilege. *The Atlantic*. https://www.theatlantic.com/personal/archive/2012/04/white-privilege/256478/. Accessed December 11, 2017.

Deonna, J. A., Rodogno, R., & Teroni, F. (2012). *In Defense of Shame: The Faces of an Emotion*. Oxford: Oxford University Press.

Drury, S. (1994). *Alexandre Kojève: The Roots of Postmodern Politics*. New York: St. Martin's.

Etzioni, A. (1999). Back to the pillory? *The American Scholar, 68*: 43–50.

Fairbairn, W. R. D. (1952). The repression and the return of bad objects. In: *Psychoanalytic Studies of the Personality* (pp. 59–81). London: Routledge & Kegan Paul.

Fairbairn, W. R. D. (1958). On the nature and aims of psychoanalytic treatment. *International Journal of Psychoanalysis, 31*: 374–385.

Faulkner, J. (2010). *Dead Letters to Nietzsche, or The Necromantic Art of Reading Philosophy*. Athens, OH: Ohio University Press.

Felman, S. (1995). Education and crisis, or the vicissitudes of teaching. In: C. Caruth (Ed.), *Trauma: Explorations in Memory* (pp. 13–60). Baltimore, MD: Johns Hopkins University Press.

Felman, S., & Laub, D. (1992). *Testimony: Crises of Witnessing in Literature, Psychoanalysis, and History*. New York: Taylor & Francis.

Fleming, C. M. (2017, September 19). Harvard has shown its commitment to diversity was always a farce:

Look how it treated Michelle Jones, a once-incarcerated woman. *Vox*. https://www.vox.com/first-person/2017/9/18/16329144/harvard-michelle-jones-diversity. Accessed September 21, 2017.

Freud, S. (1917e). Mourning and melancholia. *S. E., 14*: 243–258. London: Hogarth.

Freud, S. (1921c). *Group Psychology and the Analysis of the Ego. S. E., 18*. London: Hogarth. [Reprinted New York: W. W. Norton, 1959.]

Freud, S. (1930a). *Civilization and Its Discontents. S. E., 21*. London: Hogarth. [Reprinted New York: W. W. Norton, 1961.]

Garwood, A. (1996). The holocaust and the power of powerlessness: Survivor guilt an unhealed wound. *British Journal of Psychotherapy, 13*: 243–258.

Gibson, C. (2017, August 18). Arnold Schwarzenegger tells Trump what he should have said after Charlottesville. *The Washington Post*.

https://www.washingtonpost.com/news/reliable-source/wp/2017/08/18/arnold-schwarzenegger-tells-trump-what-he-should-have-said-after-charlottesville/?utm_term=.cd1dd15d5bd5. Accessed August 30, 2017.

Godless. (2017). Written and directed by S. Frank. Netflix Originals.

Hassan, I. (1987). *The Postmodern Turn: Essays in Postmodern Theory and Culture*. Columbus, OH: Ohio State University Press.

Holocaust Encyclopedia. (n.d.). United States Holocaust Memorial Museum, Washington, DC. https://www.ushmm.org/wlc/en/article.php?ModuleId=10007392. Accessed September 1, 2017.

Jagodzinski, J. (Ed.) (2018). *Interrogating the Anthropocene: Ecology, Aesthetics, Pedagogy and the Future in Question*. New York: Palgrave.

Johnson, D. (2016). Silence is violence: Why using our voice matters. *National Association of Student Personnel Administrators: Student Affairs Administrators in Higher Education*. https://www.naspa.org/constituent-groups/posts/silence-is-violence-why-using-our-voice-matters. Accessed August 2, 2017.

Juni, S. (2016). Survivor guilt: A critical review from the lens of the Holocaust. *International Review of Victimology*, *22*: 321–337.

Kahan, D. (1996). What do alternative sanctions mean? *University of Chicago Law Review*, *63*: 591.

Kahan, D. (2006). What's really wrong with shaming sanctions. *Faculty Scholarship Series*. Paper 102. http://digitalcommons.law.yale.edu/fss_papers/102. Accessed March 28, 2018.

Kierkegaard, S. (1980). *The Sickness unto Death: A Christian Psychological Exposition of Upbuilding and Awakening*. In: H. V. Hong & E. H. Hong (Eds. and Trans.). Princeton, NJ: Princeton University Press.

Klein, M. (1937). Love, guilt, and reparation, reprinted in *Love, Guilt, and Reparation and Other Works 1921-1945*. London, Karnac, 1992.

Klein, M. (1945). The Oedipus Complex in the light of early anxieties, reprinted in *Love, Guilt, and Reparation and Other Works 1921–1945*. London, Karnac, 1992.

Klein, M. (1957). Envy and gratitude, reprinted in *Envy and Gratitude and Other Works 1946–1963*. London, Karnac, 1993.

Kohut, H. (1977). *The Restoration of the Self*. Chicago, IL: University of Chicago Press.

Kopan, T. (2016). What Donald Trump has said about Mexico and vice versa. *CNN*. http://www.cnn.com/2016/08/31/politics/donald-trump-mexico-statements/index.html. Retrieved October 22, 2017.

Kunstler, K. (2005). *The Long Emergency: Surviving the End of Oil, Climate Change, and Other Converging Catastrophes of the Twenty-First Century.* New York: Grove.

Lacan, J. (1988). *The Seminar of Jacques Lacan: Book I, Freud's Papers on Technique, 1953–54.* J. Miller (Ed.) and J. Forrester (Trans.). Cambridge: Cambridge University Press.

Lasch, C. (1984). *The Minimal Self: Psychic Survival in Troubled Times.* New York: W. W. Norton.

Lasch, C. (1995). *Haven in a Heartless World: The Family Besieged.* New York: W. W. Norton.

Le Bon, G. (2001). *The Crowd: A Study of the Popular Mind.* Kitchener, Ontario: Batoche.

Leftovers, The. (2017). Created by D. Lindelof and T. Perrotta. *HBO.*

Lerner, M. (1980). *Belief in a Just World: A Fundamental Delusion.* New York: Plenum.

Levine, D. (2011). *The Capacity for Civic Engagement: Public and Private Worlds of the Self.* New York: Palgrave.

Levine, D. (2017). *Psychoanalysis, Society, and the Inner World: Embedded Meaning in Politics and Social Conflict.* Abingdon, UK: Routledge.

Levine, D. (2018). *Dark Fantasy: Regressive Movements and the Search for Meaning in Politics.* London: Karnac.

Leys, R. (2000). *Trauma: A Genealogy.* Chicago, IL: University of Chicago Press.

Lyotard, J.-F. (1984). The postmodern condition: A report on knowledge. In: L. Cahoonem (Ed.), *From Modernism to Postmodernism* (pp. 259–277). Malden, MA: Blackwell, 2003.

Maske, M. (2017, September 28). After Trump attack, NFL owners supported their players. But will one hire Colin Kaepernick? *The Washington Post.* https://www.washingtonpost.com/news/sports/wp/2017/09/28/nfl-owners-locked-arms-in-solidarity-with-players-after-trumps-criticism-does-that-change-the-chances-of-colin-kaepernick-getting-a-job/?utm_term=.7a7e5fe0a7f4. Accessed September 28, 2017.

McIntosh, P. (1988). White privilege and male privilege: A personal account of coming to see correspondences through work in Women's Studies. Working Paper 189, Wellesley College Center for Research on Women, Wellesley, MA.

Merriam-Webster (2006). *Merriam Webster's Collegiate Dictionary, 11th edn.* Springfield, MA: Merriam-Webster.

Miller, A. (1997). *The Drama of the Gifted Child: The Search for the True Self* (revised edn). R. Ward (Trans.). New York: Basic Books.

Mojovic, M. (2017). Untouchable infant gangs in group and social matrices as obstacles to reconciliation. In: G. Ofer (Ed.), *A Bridge Over Troubled Water: Conflicts and Reconciliation in Groups and Society*. London: Karnac.

Naas, M. (2015). *The End of the World and Other Teachable Moments: Jacques Derrida's Final Seminar*. New York: Fordham University Press.

Niederland, W. (1981). The survivor syndrome: Further observations and dimensions. *Journal of the American Psychoanalytic Association, 29*: 413–425.

Nussbaum, M. (2004). *Hiding from Humanity: Disgust, Shame and the Law*. Princeton, NJ: Princeton University Press.

Orwell, G. (1949). *Nineteen Eighty-Four*. New York: Harcourt.

Perrotta, T. (2011). *The Leftovers*. London: Harper Collins.

Popular Mechanics. (2018). 64 things to do before the world ends. *Popular Mechanics, 195*: 82–95.

Racker, H. (1968). *Transference and Countertransference*. Madison, CT: International Universities Press.

Reilly, K. (2016, July 2). Read Elie Wiesel's Nobel Peace Prize acceptance speech. *Time*. http://time.com/4392267/elie-wiesel-dead-nobel-peace-prize-speech. Accessed July 5, 2017.

Rothman, J. (2014, May 12). The origins of "privilege". *New Yorker*. https://www.newyorker.com/books/page-turner/the-origins-of-privilege. Accessed December 9, 2017.

Sehgal, P. (2015, July 14). How "privilege" became a provocation *New York Times*. https://www.nytimes.com/2015/07/19/magazine/how-privilege-became-a-provocation.html. Accessed December 9, 2017.

Spence, D. (1982). *Narrative Truth and Historical Truth: Meaning and Interpretation in Psychoanalysis*. New York: W. W. Norton.

Stein, H. (2017). *Listening Deeply: An Approach to Understanding and Consulting in Organizational Culture* (2nd edn). Columbia, MO: University of Missouri Press.

Steiner, J. (1993). *Psychic Retreats: Pathological Organizations in Psychotic, Neurotic and Borderline Patients*. London: Routledge.

Tarnopolsky, C. (2010). *Prudes, Perverts, and Tyrants: Plato's Gorgias and the Politics of Shame*. Princeton, NJ: Princeton University Press.

Tea, K. (2017). To my friends who are sick of politics. *Motherwise* [weblog]. https://motherwiselife.org/to-my-friends-who-are-sick-of-politics/. Accessed January 20, 2018.

Terr, L. (1988). What happens to early memories of trauma? A study of twenty children under age five at the time of documented traumatic events. *Journal of the American Academy of Child and Adolescent Psychiatry, 27*: 96–104.

The Washington Post. (2017). Washington Post: What trump should have said, reprinted in the *Omaha World-Herald*, August 17, 2017. http://www.omaha.com/opinion/washington-post-what-trump-should-have-said/article_9eb2aa50-8072-11e7-9075-fbeb303beb2c.html. Accessed August 30, 2017.

Wiesel, E. (2006). *Night*. M. Wiesel (Trans.). New York: Farrar, Straus & Giroux.

Winnicott, D. W. (1958a). Psycho-analysis and the sense of guilt. In: *The Maturational Process and the Facilitating Environment: Studies in the Theory of Emotional Development*. Madison, CT: International Universities Press, 1965.

Winnicott, D. W. (1958b). The capacity to be alone. In: *The Maturational Process and the Facilitating Environment: Studies in the Theory of Emotional Development*. Madison, CT: International Universities Press, 1965.

Winnicott, D. W. (1962). Providing for the child in health and in crisis. In: *The Maturational Process and the Facilitating Environment: Studies in the Theory of Emotional Development*. Madison, CT: International Universities Press, 1965.

Winnicott, D. W. (1965). Ego distortions in terms of true and false self. In: *The Maturational Process and the Facilitating Environment: Studies in the Theory of Emotional Development*. Madison, CT: International Universities Press, 1965.

Winnicott, D. W. (1974). Fear of breakdown. In: C. Winnicott, R. Shepherd, & M. Davis (Eds.), *Psychoanalytic Explorations* (87-95). Cambridge, MA: Harvard University Press.

Winnicott, D. W. (1986). *Home Is Where We Start from: Essays by a Psychoanalyst*. C. Winnicott, R. Shepard, & M. Davis (Eds.). New York: W. W. Norton.

Wolfe, T. (1940). *You Can't Go Home Again*. New York: Harper & Row.

Wyche, S. (2016, August 28). Colin Kaepernick explains why he sat during national anthem. *NFL.com*. http://www.nfl.com/news/story/0ap3000000691077/article/colin-kaepernick-explains-why-he-sat-during-national-anthem. Accessed October 1, 2017.

Žižek, S. (2011). *Living in the End Times*. London: Verso.

Index